HOW SOUTH ASIANS HELPED TO MAKE HONG KONG

$\longrightarrow$

History
Culture
Profiles
Food
Shopping

Written by $\rightarrow$

Mark O'Neill, Annemarie Evans

Photographs by $\rightarrow$

Kevin On Man Lee

Coordinator $\rightarrow$

HARTCO

A diversity of many races and cultures
that has formed the Hong Kong of today.

Introduction

When a visitor arrives for the first time in Hong Kong, it is clear this is a Chinese city, but with a Western overlay. The faces are mostly Chinese, the conversations are likely in the unfamiliar tones of the Cantonese dialect and Chinese characters abound. But English is also seen and heard. At the arrival hall at the city's airport, there are usually more than a few Caucasians, many of them residents waiting to greet visiting relatives and friends. These first impressions are a reminder that while Hong Kong is now part of China, it was a British colony for 156 years. The city boasts a cultural mix that combines Chinese cuisine, temples, mahjong and tai chi with colonial buildings, law courts, cricket and afternoon tea. The city's newspapers, magazines and television programmes all underscore this historical mix, delivering their messages in Chinese and English alike.

But this is not the whole story. Hong Kong is a city not only of Chinese and British but of many nationalities. According to the 2016 census, eight per cent of its 7.35 million people – or 584,000 – were not Chinese. The largest group, some 348,000, were from Indonesia, Thailand and the Philippines, most of them employed as domestic maids. The second largest group were some 80,000 South Asians from India, Pakistan, Nepal, Bangladesh and Sri Lanka. This second group are the subject of our book.

They occupy a special place in the history of Hong Kong. Many of their families have been in the city longer than those of the Chinese who live here. When Captain Charles Elliot raised the British flag over Hong Kong on January 26, 1841, there were more than 2,700 Indians on hand to witness the historic event. They were soldiers and merchants — soldiers from the regiments of the British Indian Army and merchants who were Parsees from Western India. For the next 100 years, Indians played an essential role in the development and security of the colony. They worked not only as soldiers, but also as police, prison guards and security men. They ran international trading firms that shipped Chinese tea, silk, porcelain and spices to India and the West in exchange for opium, cotton, garments and other goods. They sold diamonds and jewellery. Of the 13 founding committee members of the Hong Kong and Shanghai Banking Corporation in 1864, two were Indian Parsees and one an Indian Jew. An Indian Parsee founded the Star Ferry while another Indian Parsee was a proponent of and key donor to the University of Hong Kong, the city's first institution of tertiary education. A third built the Rutonjee Sanatorium in Wan Chai — named after him — to combat tuberculosis.

The Hong Kong police force in 1906 consisted of 1,050 men — 128 Europeans, 511 Chinese and 411 Indians. Indian soldiers paid a heavy price in World War Two, helping to defend the colony from invading Japanese forces in December 1941. At least 100 were killed and thousands taken prisoner for the duration of the war. The Nepalis came to Hong Kong in 1969-70 as Gurkhas in the British Army. They were given the job of guarding the border with China, keeping out illegal immigrants.

When Hong Kong became a major industrial centre in the 1970s and 1980s, Indian trading firms played an invaluable role, accounting for as much as 10 per cent of the city's gross domestic product. Local firms were able to produce a large volume of quality products

– but did not have the language or financial tools to deliver them to foreign clients. Indian firms had the global contacts and financial networks to do this. In particular, these contacts were instrumental in trade with developing countries. South Asians made tailoring one of their favoured professions. Visitors to Hong Kong are still able to order a custom-made suit that is cut and fitted within 24 hours. South Asians also worked as doctors, teachers, engineers and in other professions. And for many years, no major construction project has been undertaken in the city without the help of their labour.

South Asians brought with them their languages, religion, sports, customs, festivals and food. These have been preserved here until today. They built temples, mosques and other places of worship. Their sports and recreation clubs gave them a place to play cricket and hockey and the restaurants they opened offered a dazzling array of culinary styles and dishes – from curries and halal meat to vegan and vegetarian fare.

Our book aims to introduce the history, religion, traditions, customs and experiences of the South Asians of Hong Kong. It describes the products they sell and the food they serve. We hope that it will inspire readers – residents of Hong Kong and visitors alike – to open their eyes wider and see this rich diversity around them and experience it for themselves. This city belongs to many people, from diverse backgrounds.

——————————— Mark O'Neill

→ *Contents*

12   Chapter 1 ⟶ Indians – Here Since the Foundation of Hong Kong

68   Chapter 2 ⟶ The Muslims of Hong Kong

116   Chapter 3 ⟶ Sikhs – Lions and Princesses from the Punjab

140   Chapter 4 ⟶ Gurkhas – Protecting the Border, Keeping the Peace

172   Chapter 5 ⟶ Sri Lankans – Travellers from the Tear Drop Nation

190   Chapter 6 ⟶ Textiles, Bengali Culture and Islam

206   Chapter 7 ⟶ From Momos to Masala – South Asian Food in Hong Kong

242   Chapter 8 ⟶ Tailors, Beauticians and Jewellers

280   Chapter 9 ⟶ The Sporting Life

296   Chapter 10 ⟶ From Fasting to Feasting – South Asian Festivals

314   Acknowledgements

317   Photo Credits

Indians – Here Since the Foundation of Hong Kong

Indians – Here Since the Foundation of Hong Kong

Indians have been part of Hong Kong since it was founded in 1841. Over the years they have been an important part of the fabric of life in the city, working as international traders, diamond merchants, soldiers, policemen and tailors. They have likewise made their mark in law, medicine and finance and taken important roles in the government. In the 1990s, Indians made up less than half a percent of the population but their businesses accounted for as much as nine per cent of the city's global trade. The community today numbers about 45,000 - almost doubling in size since the handover to China in 1997. For the most part the new arrivals have been professionals – engineers and professors as well as workers in finance and IT, alongside the more traditional fields of diamonds and jewellery, shipping and trade.

Indians brought with them their languages and customs as well as

→ The Capture of a Notorious Chinese Pirate, Chang Yeh, at Hong Kong, *London Illustrated Newspaper*, 1887.

religion, music and dance. By and large they have retained their cultural links, maintaining close ties with Indian communities around the world and forming an intricate network that has helped make Hong Kong Asia's world city. These Indian communities have traditionally been close-knit – with most young people marrying within their own group.

→ *History*

Indians were an essential part of Britain's imperial army. When the British flag was raised over Hong Kong in January 1841, at least 2,700

→ (Top) The main Central Police Station, consisting of a Barrack Block and a parade ground, was built in 1864. The building provides accommodation for the growing number of police constables, including many Sikh policemen.

→ (Bottom) Management of prison guards was transferred from the police department to the Superintendent of the Gaol, 1879.

Indian soldiers – and four Indian merchants – were there to witness the historic event. Even before the colony was founded, Indian firms were trading with China, many of them dealing in the lucrative – though debilitating – commodity of the time – opium. The British wanted Hong Kong for its excellent deep-water harbour, the best on the south China coast, and that led to its emergence as a shipping and trading centre.

Indians played a key role in making the colony into a trading and shipping powerhouse. Of the 13 founding committee members of the Hongkong and Shanghai Banking Corporation in 1864, two were Indian Parsees and one an Indian Jew. In 1888, an Indian Parsee founded the Star Ferry, which still shuttles across the harbour carrying commuters and sightseers alike. Ebrahim Noordin, a Muslim from Surat on the west coast of India, founded Abdoolally Ebrahim in 1842; it is the oldest Indian firm in Hong Kong and is still in business today. By June 1845, there were 362 Indians and 595 Europeans living in Hong Kong, out of a total population of 23,817.

Indians were also a vital part of Hong Kong's security forces. Prior to World War Two, one-third of the police force was Indian, mostly Sikhs from Punjab. Many other Indians served in the British military and prison services. In December 1941, Indian soldiers served

→ From 1861, Hong Kong police recruited members from India, first from Mumbai and later Sikhs from the Punjab region. Sikh police officers were allowed to retain their customs and religion – they wore turbans, instead of police caps, and were assigned a room where they could shower before prayers.

gallantly in resisting invading Japanese forces. During the Japanese occupation, large numbers of Indians were interned in prison camps around the British colony. By February 1942, there were 10,947 prisoners of war in Hong Kong and 3,329 of them were Indian. In Happy Valley, there is a Commonwealth War Graves Commission memorial to one Sikh and eight Hindu soldiers who died in the defence of Hong Kong; the Muslim Cemetery there contains the graves of 24 Muslims from the Indian sub-continent who lost their lives in World War One and Two.

→ *Star Ferry*

One of the most visible Indian contributions to the former British colony is the Star Ferry, which has operated a passenger service between Hong Kong Island and the Kowloon peninsula for 130 years. Almost every visitor takes the iconic ferry at least once during a visit to Hong Kong – no matter how short. Despite the alternative of the underground train, which shuttles briskly beneath the harbour, the ferry is still widely used, offering spectacular views, a refreshing sea breeze and a few minutes of tranquility amid the city's frenetic workday pace. The ferries carry over 52,851 passengers a day or 19.3 million a year. In 2009, a poll by the Society of American Travel Writers rated the Star Ferry first among the "Top 10 Most Exciting Ferry Rides" in the world.

In 1888, businessman Dorabjee Naorojee Mithaiwalas founded the "Kowloon Ferry Company" and acquired three boats to carry passengers across the harbour. The service was so successful that a fourth vessel was purchased. Each had the word "Star" in its name, and the following year the firm was renamed the "Star Ferry". That familiar name is still in use today. Each boat could carry 100 passengers, with an average of 147 crossings a day at that time. On his retirement in 1898, Naorojee sold the company to the Hong Kong and Kowloon Wharf and Godown Company, owned at that time by Jardine, Matheson & Co and Sir Catchick Paul Chater, a prominent British-Indian businessman of Armenian descent. Until the opening of the first cross-harbour tunnel in 1972, the Star Ferry

→ The first pier of the Star Ferry, 1902.

was the main form of public transportation linking Hong Kong island and Kowloon.

Naorojee arrived in Hong Kong in 1852; he stowed away on a ship bound for China from Bombay (now Mumbai), finding work on board as a cook. He set out on his own in the business world, initially selling opium to China. Eventually, his main interest – besides operating ferries – would be managing hotels. Ultimately, he ran four of them. After he retired to India in 1898, he passed management of the hotels to his son.

→ *Bank, University & Hospital*

Naorojee was a Parsee (meaning Persia). Parsees are followers of

→ The priest of the Parsees in Hong Kong performs his daily ritual.

Zoroastrianism, one of the world's oldest living religions, originally from what is now Iran. Zoroastrianism entered recorded history in the fifth century B.C. It was the state religion of pre-Islamic Parsee for more than 1,000 years, losing that role after the Muslim conquest in the mid-seventh century A.D. After the conversion of the population to Islam, many Zoroastrians fled to escape persecution and settled in western India. The community made great contributions to the modernisation of their new homeland. In more recent years they built factories, mills, steel plants, hospitals, hotels, and educational and research institutes. They were also prominent in philanthropy. The Tatas, one of the biggest industrial and commercial families of India, are Parsees; their community helped make Mumbai the industrial and commercial capital of India.

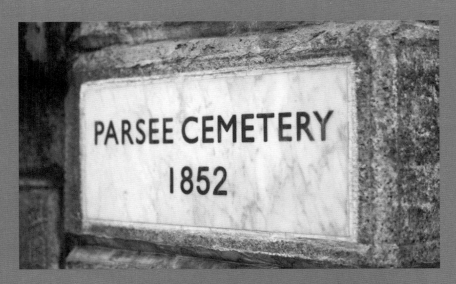

The Parsees first arrived in China in the mid-18th century, settling in Macau and Guangzhou (then known to the West as Canton). They built trading houses that dealt in spices, opium, silk and cotton. When the British flag was raised over Hong Kong on January 26, 1841, three of the four Indian merchant firms represented were Parsees. They have made a major contribution to the city in the years since. As mentioned above, two of the 13 founding members of the Hongkong and Shanghai Bank were Parsees. In the 1860s, there were 17 Parsee-owned firms listed in the Hong Kong Directory.

In 1861, a Parsee named Sir Hormusjee Noarojee Mody arrived in Hong Kong to work for an Indian banker and opium trader. He set up his own opium trading operation and later expanded into other businesses. In 1889, he built the Prince's Building and Queen's Building, now the Mandarin Oriental, in Hong Kong's Central district. He was a prime mover in the establishment of the University of Hong Kong, the city's oldest and most famous institution of higher learning. In 1907, he offered to put up the buildings for HK$150,000 and donated an additional HK$30,000 for an endowment fund, substantial sums at the time. With the help of other donations, the university was built in late 1911 and opened in March 1912. He died too soon to see his project come to fruition but, in tribute to his generosity, a bronze bust of him graces one of

→ A bust of Sir Hormusjee Noarojee Mody sits inside Loke Yew Hall at the University of Hong Kong.

the main buildings. In a report on March 11, 1912, the *South China Morning Post* said of him: "The one great ambition of his life was to place within the reach of others what, through force of circumstances, he himself had been denied in his youth. The university will be open to all races and creeds, and no student will be compelled to study any particular form of religion, in which respect it resembles Oxford and Cambridge and other Western universities." Mody was also a benefactor of the Kowloon Cricket Club and served as its first president. Mody Road in Tsim Sha Tsui, home to numerous Indian tailors, restaurants and retail shops, is named after him. Bisney Road and Kotewall Road are also named after famous Parsees.

In 1949, in the Wan Chai district, a new hospital opened – the Ruttonjee Sanatorium. The main donor was Jehangir Hormusjee

→ Ruttonjee Hospital in Wan Chai district.

Ruttonjee, who made his generous gift in memory of his daughter, Tehmi Ruttonjee-Desai, who had died of tuberculosis in 1943. He was also a Parsee who founded a family business in Hong Kong in 1887. The Ruttonjee Sanatorium was one of the main institutions treating tuberculosis in Hong Kong. In 1991, as the number of TB patients declined, it was converted into the Ruttonjee Hospital, a 600-bed facility, with a wide range of health services to meet the needs of the community. It has become an acute general hospital with general medical and surgical specialities. Its acclaimed surgical department has made Ruttonjee the only hospital in Hong Kong to perform sex-change operations. The geriatrics services have gained renown in recent years, providing needed services to the ageing population of Wan Chai.

The priest of the Parsees in Hong Kong today is Homyar G. Nasirabadwala, who is in his 60s. Each day, inside the Zoroastrian Building in Causeway Bay, he performs a ritual that originated in ancient Parsee. Dressed in white, with a veil covering part of his face, he prays in front of a burning fire five times a day. Hong Kong's Zoroastrian temple dates back to 1842.

The Happy Valley district is also home to the Parsee cemetery. Over the last 70 years, the Parsee community in India as well as Hong Kong has dwindled. In India, the number of Parsees has fallen from 114,000 in the 1940s to 57,000 as of the 2011 census. This decline reflects the marrying of Parsee women outside the community and the trend towards having fewer children. Strict rules also make conversion into the faith difficult. In Hong Kong the Parsees now number about 250.

→ *The Indian Armenian "Father of Hong Kong"*

Alongside Parsee entrepreneurs who helped found modern Hong Kong, was Sir Catchick Paul Chater. He was also a philanthropist, and passionate throroughbred horse racer, who came to Hong Kong as an orphaned child to join his older sister, was the main driver behind a number of leading Hong Kong firms and early efforts at land reclamation. His obituary in the *South China Morning Post* on 28 May 1926 stated that:"A biography of Sir Catchick Paul Chater would be a history of Hong Kong."

Chater became an orphan at the age of seven. In 1864, at the age of 18, he came to Hong Kong to join an older sister, and initially he worked in a bank. There are some wonderful stories about Chater, how he went out in Victoria Harbour at night in a sampan to test the water depth to implement his plans for reclamation. He founded or co-founded around 20 companies, including the brokerage company Chater & Mody with his close friend, Sir Homusjee Mody; Dairy Farm; Hongkong Land and Kowloon Wharf and Godown, the predecessor of The Wharf (Holdings) Ltd. He was behind the Praya Reclamation Scheme in 1890, and later the creation of Hongkong Electric.

→ A plaque of Sir Catchick Paul Chater at the entrance of Chater House in Central.

Chater was a legislator, an executive councillor and senior justice of the peace. He was a major art collector and served as the chairman of the Hong Kong Jockey Club for 30 years. He financed the construction of St Andrew's Church in Tsim Sha Tsui solely through his own funds.

Chater propelled Hong Kong forward. He envisioned what Kowloon and the New Territories could become. Some of his famous Chater Collection of oil paintings, water colours, sketches, prints and photographs still exists today, though some of it was lost during the Japanese military occupation of Hong Kong. These days in Hong Kong, his name can be found at Chater Road, Chater House, where his bronze bust is in the lobby, and Chater Garden. When he died in 1926, he bequeathed his home, Marble Hall, and all its contents to the Hong Kong Government.

→ *Indian Schools*

In 1891, Ellis Kadoorie, a Jewish businessman and philanthropist, opened a school for the children of Indian residents of Hong Kong. Known as the "Ellis Kadoorie School for Indians", it was the first school in the city which included the Hindi and Urdu languages in its curriculum. This school symbolised both the generosity of Ellis Kadoorie and the fact that Indian children were not well served by an education system that catered to Western expatriates and local Chinese. The school was supported by wealthy Indians, as well as the Kadoorie and Arculli families, both of which had strong ties to India. Kadoorie decided to donate the school to the government. Governor Henry May presided at the official opening of the new school on October 16, 1916. The report of the director of education for that year said: "The building is very suitable and the playgrounds are, by the standards of the Colony, luxurious. An English Master has been appointed." Like many schools in the city, it was closed during World War Two. After the war, it reopened and lives on today, on a new site in West Kowloon. It remains a government-run school, with English as the main teaching medium. It is multi-racial and has students of many nationalities. Studying Chinese is required and students may take Hindi, Urdu and French as elective subjects.

Today, the school's website has this to say: "Our school was first established at a site in Sai Ying Poon through the generosity of the Kadoorie Family in the 1890s. The Hong Kong Government assumed the school management in 1916 and the school later moved to its old site at Eastern Hospital Road. For many years, it was operated as a primary school until the 1960s with the introduction of the secondary classes. It has remained a government co-educational secondary school ever since. At the beginning of the new millennium, the school has moved into its present site, a new and very well facilitated school building with the latest modern design, progressing onwards with strength and vitality into new era ahead. Appreciating the cultural diversity of the students and reflecting

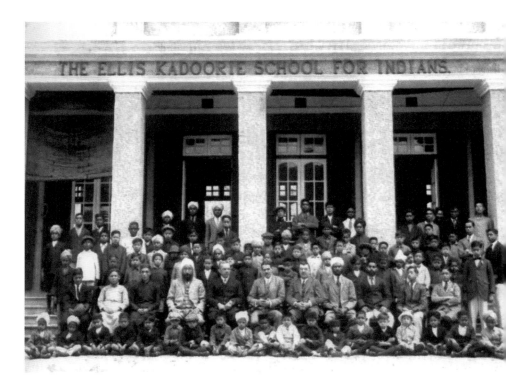

→ The Ellis Kadoorie School for Indians, 1916.

on the changing demands of the modern world, the school aims at the holistic development of all students in order to enable them to become lifelong learners, and valuable members of the local and global community." Its students include Indians, Pakistanis, Nepalis, Filipinos, and Thais, among others. In Hong Kong, there are over 10,000 school-age children of the South Asian community.

→ *Police*

One of the most important roles for Indians in the new colony was in the police force. Initially, the force consisted of British officers and Punjabi, Sikh and Muslim constables. Chinese constables were recruited later. Hong Kong had a police force of 1,050 in 1906; there were 128 Europeans, 511 Chinese and 411 Indians. Europeans

Chapter 1 —— Indians – Here Since the Foundation of Hong Kong

→ (Top) Allah Dad Ditta, son of Allah Ditta (1913-1980), holds his father's ID as an Indian policeman in the Royal Navy Yard in Hong Kong. His name was printed incorrectly.

→ (Bottom) Allah Dad Ditta holds the medals his father received as a soldier in Hong Kong. He fought the Japanese in World War Two. They include the 1939-45 Star; the Pacific Star; and the 1929-45 Defence Medal.

held the senior positions while Chinese and Indians made up the rank and file. While the European officers could rise as high as superintendent, the highest rank the Chinese and Indians could aspire to was sergeant. The British recruited Sikhs from the Punjab, considering them to be brave, strong and loyal. Like the whites, they were foreigners whose loyalty to the crown could be relied on in times of crisis. They usually had a better command of English than Chinese constables. The British assigned them to different quarters to those of their Chinese colleagues so the groups tended not to mix socially. In 1927, the police force was comprised of 246 Europeans, 753 Indians and 816 Chinese. After India's Partition in 1947, the force continued to recruit Muslim Punjabis, citizens of the new country of Pakistan. The last contingent, of 46, arrived in 1961.

→ *Soldiers*

As stated earlier, the first South Asians to arrive in Hong Kong were Indian soldiers who accompanied their British officers in 1841. For the next century, Indian soldiers – Hindu, Sikh and Muslim – served in the British army in Hong Kong and elsewhere around the world. That tradition ended when India won its independence in 1947, and Britain was no longer able to recruit Indians as soldiers. In addition to the army, Indians were members of the Hong Kong police force and worked as private security guards, playing a key role in maintaining law and order in the British colony. The 1901 census listed 202 non-Chinese watchmen in the colony alongside 177 Chinese. According to the 1931 census, there were 3,475 Indians in Hong Kong; 1,270 of them were in the army and 398 were members of the police force. Another 127 were in the civil service and 1,294 in trade and commerce, while 108 were professionals and 34 worked as domestic or personal servants. The rest were listed as guards, watchmen or lay priests.

→ *International Trade*

International trade was another sector in which Indians played an important role in the new colony. The establishment of British rule and political stability opened new economic opportunities for trade with China and other countries in East Asia. The first to come from India – besides Parsees – were Bohra Muslims. They were followed by Sindhis and Gujaratis, both of these groups being Hindus from western India. They traded with China, dealing in cotton, silk and opium, and they opened stores that sold goods to the British soldiers stationed in Hong Kong. In 1898, there were 1,348 Indians in Hong Kong. By the 1960s, it was 20,000.

Religion, race, customs and language set the South Asians apart from the local Chinese population. Those who needed to interact frequently with local people learnt Cantonese. But the two had limited contact outside work and business. This was because both sides favoured marriages that remained within their own communities. Hindus, Sikhs and Muslims generally wanted to preserve their own religion, language and customs. Parents in these communities often opposed marriages across religious and racial lines – and much like their Chinese neighbours – were reluctant to see inter-racial alliances. Ties to the local community – the centre of their social and religious life – were extremely important. Their native land was under the control of Britain, a foreign power, and an independent India was decades away.

British residents of Hong Kong often had the same view of the need to maintain racial purity. Government institutions and even the biggest firms often insisted that young British men who wanted a lifetime career should marry someone of their own race and educate their children in British schools, in Hong Kong or at home. The British brought to their colonies the class system of the mother country. In this system, Indians had their place between the British rulers and the Chinese population.

→ Worshippers take part in the regular Sunday worship at the Hindu Temple of Hong Kong in Happy Valley.

→ *The Hindu Temple*

The religious, cultural and social centre of Hinduism in Hong Kong is the Hindu temple in Happy Valley. Hong Kong is home to 120,000 Hindus, most of them from India, Nepal, Sri Lanka, and the island of Bali in Indonesia. The temple was built by the Hindu Association, which was established in 1949. The colonial government assigned land in the district to different religious groups to build cemeteries. It gave the land to the Hindu community in 1928, initially for burials. But Hindus cremate their dead rather than bury them. With an amendment in the terms of land use, the community built the temple on the site. The foundation stone was laid on February 15, 1953, and the temple was inaugurated on September 13 of that year.

The temple is a three-storey building, divided into six bays separated by columns. The architectural style is Indian, but with evidence of Western influence. The roof is flat, with a dome at the southeast end. The focus of the complex is the worship hall. Its walls are adorned with plaques displaying the names of those who have been key financial supporters. It is a very distinctive building, looking out over Happy Valley's hugely popular race course and proudly proclaiming the long history of the Hindu community in the city. Before its construction, Hindus worshipped with local Sikhs at the nearby Gurudwara (Sikh temple). "The government gave us the land and the believers provided the money to build the temple," said Lal Hardasani, acting president of the temple management committee, in an interview. "The majority of the community then and now is Sindhis." In addition to the Sindhis, the Hindu community in Hong Kong includes Gujaratis, Marwaris, Bengalis, Punjabis, Nepalis, South Indians and Balinese.

"The architecture is that of a normal temple in India," said Lal. "The dome indicates that it is a temple. The building includes quarters for a priest with two bedrooms, a bathroom and a kitchen. The priests have always come from India. We prefer to have a married one, so that he is not lonely." Sham Kewlani, 40, is the current priest. He is married and hails from Mumbai. Since 1953, there have been more than a dozen priests. Religious services are usually in Hindi, the national language of India that is understood by the largest number of people, though English is also used.

The main days of worship are Sunday and Monday. On Sunday, about 150-200 worshippers attend, with 600-800 on major festivals like Shivratri, celebrated to honour the god Shiva. The religious service is followed by a community meal that is free to all who wish to attend. Another important festival is Diwali, the Hindu festival of lights celebrated in the northern hemisphere autumn. In Hong Kong, the Indian consul-general is traditionally asked to attend. Other important festivals are Holi, the Birth of Lord Krishna, and Dussehra. The temple is frequently visited by swamis and learned men from overseas who lecture on spiritual matters. The temple is

→ Devotees of Hinduism donate money during Sunday worship at Happy Valley Hindu Temple on 18 March 2018.

also licensed by the government to perform marriages, though in recent years, many Indians have favoured "destination weddings", opting for the beaches of Koh Samui and Phuket in Thailand and Bali in Indonesia. Twice a month the temple receives groups of local students who come to learn about Hinduism. "Hinduism is not a religion but a way of life," says Lal. "There are many Gods to pray to. We respect all religions." He adds that after 65 years, the temple is showing some wear and tear. "Fortunately, the community is generous."

The Hindu Association is also responsible for arranging cremations for the Hindu community at the Cape Collison cemetery in Chai Wan; the crematorium is managed by the government. "We prefer cremation within 24 hours," says Lal. "But mostly they are within 48 hours. If a person dies at home, the government requires a post-mortem, which takes 2-3 days. We charge nothing for all the services needed for one who has passed away."

At the Chai Wan cemetery, there are 12 cremation furnaces, one reserved for the Hindu community, thanks to the efforts of F.T. Melwani, the first president of the association. "We believe in reincarnation until you achieve salvation and go to paradise," says Lal. After cremation, the government grinds the ashes and gives them to the family. Some scatter them in the sea; others take them to India and scatter them in the Ganges or other holy rivers. The temple in Happy Valley is open between 0900 and 1300 hours and 1600 and 2000 hours each day. Individual visitors are welcome during these hours. Groups are asked to make arrangements in advance.

There is one other Hindu temple in Kowloon, on the second floor of an apartment building in Carnavon Road in Tsim Sha Tsui. It originally belonged to the Harilela family which donated it to the Incorporated Trustees of Hindu Mandir, so that everyone could use it. Since most Indians live in Hung Hom, Homantin, Tsim Sha Tsui and other districts of Kowloon, this temple is particularly convenient for them. In addition, there are a few Hindu centres, like the Chinmaya Mission and the Sathya Sai Baba Centre of Hong Kong, which provide classes in Hinduism for children.

"Most of us have a small temple in our home," says Lal. "Each evening we perform Arti," he says, referring to a ceremony of worship to the deities, in which the devotee has an offering tray with a lighted oil diva lamp, burning incense and a small bell. "We pass family values to our children. We ask them to be vegetarian each Monday and Thursday of the week, wherever they are in the world. We prefer that our children marry within our community, but it is not easy. They go abroad to study and fall in love. But without cultural similarity, it is difficult to sustain a marriage."

→ *The Contribution of Indians to Hong Kong*

Lal Hardasani is Sindhi. The Sindhi community is the largest group of Indians in Hong Kong, numbering 16,000 to 18,000. "Some Indian families have been here since the 1840s," says Lal. "The Sindhis came later in the 1920s and 1930s; they were active in tailoring and in the trade of silk. British women loved silk fabrics, so the Sindhi traders bought them from China and India and supplied them to the British market. Indians here also worked as tailors for the British army and British residents, as well as the local community."

The Partition of British India in 1947 was a tragedy for Sindh province. While the provinces of Punjab and Bengal were divided between India and Pakistan, all of Sindh was given to the new Muslim state of Pakistan. Sindhis are Hindus and many felt that they had no place in the new state. "One million Sindhis departed. They left everything behind and had to start a new life from zero. Partition was a disaster for us. Fortunately, we are a hard-working community. We have prospered through integrity and hard work. We were like Germany and Japan (after their defeat), we rose again from the ashes. In India, Sindhis built many colleges and modern hospitals, mainly in Bombay. A survey by Forbes in 2014 found that, out of the 100 billionaires in India, 89 were Sindhis, although we account for less than 0.5 per cent of the population."

The exodus following Partition drew Sindhis to far off destinations such as Nigeria, Panama, Japan and Hong Kong. The Sindhis have a long tradition of global business, and this meant that the Sindhi traders in Hong Kong had access to a global network of contacts and capital. "In the 1990s, Indians accounted for nine per cent of Hong Kong's international trade even though we were not half a per cent of the population," said Lal. "Trading is in our blood. Many markets were opened by Indians. In the 1950s and 1960s, there were many factories in Hong Kong producing shoes, sports goods and clothes. Their owners could not speak or read English. We acted as middlemen for them and did the paperwork for both them and the buyers." Wyndham Street in Central was once full of Indian import-export firms.

→ Parekh House in Wyndham Street. The street has been home to many Indian firms.

→ Dhanraj Ghale delivers takeaways for restaurants. He arrived Hong Kong 21 years ago.

Lal says that his community is an integral part of Hong Kong's history. "We are part of its growth. It has become our home now. We go to India and are happy to visit. But our home is here. We never felt any racism or persecution in Hong Kong. It is a harmonious society. As long as you offer something positive, you are welcome. Even during the wars between India and Pakistan, we had meals with our Pakistani friends here. These wars are created by politicians. We have been well treated by the government, both before and after the handover. The government consults the Indian Chamber of Commerce over trade issues."

The composition of the community has changed since the handover in 1997. Lal said that a few departed before 1997, emigrating to India, Canada and Australia. "They told me later that there were better business opportunities here. Under the British, there were about 500 Indians in the civil service. The number is down to 50-100 now. A good knowledge of Cantonese is essential, but many ethnic minorities are only taught a simple level of it in school." Over the last 10 years, thousands of new Indian migrants have come to Hong Kong, to work as engineers, professors, in the diamond and jewellery trade, in shipping and as professionals in banks, IT and insurance. Trading remains the most important occupation. "You can get a visa if you bring money, open companies and create employment, if you are a manager or have qualifications that are not available locally. What the government does not want is unqualified workers."

→ *Indian Chamber of Commerce*

International trade has always been a focus of Hong Kong's Indian communities. On December 12, 1952, 10 business leaders set up the Indian Chamber of Commerce in Hong Kong, to represent the interests of all Indian traders in the colony. They played an important role in the growing trade with India. In the 1950s, many Indian businessmen migrated to Hong Kong as Sino-Indian trade flourished. After the city became an important manufacturing centre and its economy boomed, these traders, both Hindu and Muslim, prospered and their status rose. The chamber has been serving the community ever since and now has about 500 members. It lists among its objectives: promoting and protecting the trade, commerce, shipping and manufacture of Hong Kong and South China: and representing and expressing the views of the Indian community on matters of commercial interest, including in terms of legislation. It is an interface between the Indian business community and the government of the Special Administrative Region of Hong Kong.

Raj Sital is president of the Council of Hong Kong Indian Associations. (Its members are the Indian Chamber of Commerce HK, the India Association HK, the Hindu Association, the India Club, the HK Indian Women's Club, the Khalsa Diwan, the Nav Bharat Club, the Non-Resident Indian Association of Hong Kong and the Overseas Indian Organisation).

→ Ray Sital is President of the Hong Kong Council of Indian Associations.

"This council was founded 40 years ago by Hari Harilela," he says. "It includes nine member associations, which include social, economic and religious bodies. One year before he passed away, Dr Harilela nominated me as president. There are about 1,000 – 1,200 Indian companies in Hong Kong. The Indian Chamber of Commerce (ICC) has over 500 companies. Of these, 50-60 per cent are local Indian firms, whose families have been here for two to three generations. About 20 per cent are Hong Kong branches of large Indian companies and about 20 per cent are individual members, mostly professionals working for large companies. Indians are very strong in ship management; many firms in this field have an Indian CEO. The ICC is a local, not a foreign chamber of commerce, like the American Chamber of Commerce. It has the right to issue 'certificates of origin' documents. But it does not have a seat in LegCo, (the Legislative Council, or local legislature) unlike the other four local chambers of commerce.

"As of 2013, Indian companies accounted for about eight per cent of Hong Kong's GDP; now the figure has fallen to less than five per cent. Our strength has been in our networks in markets like Africa, South America, East Europe, Middle East, Commonwealth of Independent States countries and Asia. We finance the trade of manufacturers in Hong Kong and the mainland who are selling to customers in these markets that do not have convertible currencies. These manufacturers are unable to give credit to a customer when it takes 45-60 days to ship the product. We are able to do this, because we have contacts in these countries."

Mr Sital is proud of the contribution by Indians throughout Hong Kong's history. "The Star Ferry was founded by an Indian." he says. Of the first board of 10 to 12 members of HSBC, three were Indians. One of the founders of HK University was Indian. Our tradition is to give back through philanthropy. The Harilelas are very generous. In terms of sectors of the economy, our contribution has been in trading: real estate: garments, textiles and tailoring. The Parsees have been here since the very beginning.

"In the Partition, the whole of Sindh province was included in Pakistan. Some of the Hindu Sindhis preferred to migrate to places in the British empire, such as Hong Kong, Singapore, Ghana, Nigeria, Gibraltar and Belize, where they had freedom of movement. Their first act on arrival was to buy property – homes, shops and businesses. If you have real estate, any bank will lend to you. Tailoring was a very important profession for the Indians, of which Sam's Tailor is the most famous. Now the young people do not wish to do it. So the measuring is done in Hong Kong and the suits are made in Shenzhen.

"In the 1960s and 1970s, we played an important role in finding markets and providing finance for Hong Kong products. We had a global network. We marry within our community, so many people overseas were our distant relatives."

Did Indians emigrate before 1997? "A few did. But later they came back. In the property market, they had made big losses, because property prices here rose much faster than in the countries where they emigrated. Before the handover, we made many trips to Beijing and met people in the Hong Kong and Macau Affairs Office. The officials made it very clear to us that, since we were not ethnic Chinese, we would not be given Chinese nationality. So we lobbied the British government, Governor Chris Patten, the Home Office and Parliament for full British passports for the Indians here who were stateless. I qualify for an SAR passport but would have to give up any other nationality. Chinese with foreign passports, on the other hand, have been able to obtain an SAR passport without giving up their existing passport, if that country allows more than one. India does not allow dual nationality. So, in the period before the deadline three months before the handover, many Indians gave up their passports, in order to be eligible for the full UK passport. About 20,000-30,000 Indians obtained it, 85-90 per cent of the Indians, who had British Dependent Territories Citizen (BDTC) document here. It was a very humanitarian decision; we are very content. A handful of Indians

→ An Indian shop owner nicknamed "Maxi" pictured at his jeans shop in Chungking Mansions. "Maxi" studied here and has lived in Hong Kong for 13 years.

were given full UK passports among the 50,000 which the British government gave out after June 4 (Beijing's 1989 crackdown on a pro-democracy movement in China).

"Before 1997, we were assured by the Chinese government that foreign businesses here would enjoy the same privileges and conditions as before the handover. They wanted us to know that nothing would change for 50 years. We were comfortable with that." How have things changed since 1997?

"The Indians' share of Hong Kong's GDP has fallen to about five per cent today. This is due to the aggressive financing by Chinese state banks which provide cheap credit. The Bank of China has more branches in Hong Kong than HSBC. This financing has led to more competition for our firms from mainland firms and Hong Kong companies which can get credit from mainland banks. The Bank of China and ICBC are courting us too. We are reliable and our default rate is very low. As a result, some of the small trading companies have closed. The younger people do not want to work in them. They want to be professionals. Most of the manufacturing is sub-contracted to the mainland. It is easier to move from one product to another, if you do not own the manufacturing yourself.

"Before 1997, the number of Indians in Hong Kong was in the low 20,000s. Now there are more than 40,000 – mostly professionals hired by large companies, such as in fleet management. If a big company applies for you, you can easily obtain a visa. After seven years, they can apply for permanent residence.

"We have received the same treatment from the SAR government as we did from the colonial government before 1997. There are now very few Indians in government service. Those who were in service in 1997 were not forced to leave and could stay on. But there was no new hiring. Before, spoken Cantonese was sufficient to become a government officer. Now writing and reading Chinese is mandatory. We have lobbied the government over this; we argue that, in jobs where written Chinese is not essential, it should hire Indians." The most senior Indians in the pre-1997 government were Ish Bhagat, a senior official of the Correctional Service Department, and Mr (Haidar) Barma, who rose to become secretary of transport.

"Historically, expatriate Indians here did not want to move back to India. There was no Indian school here. The community sent their children to international schools, so that they could go to universities abroad. But, over the last year, for the first time, there has been discussion of setting up an Indian school in Hong Kong with an Indian curriculum. This is because the economy there has improved and the standard of living has improved. Some are looking to go back. The Department of Education has asked us to provide details of this; it would be able to provide a site, as it has for other international schools here."says of Mr Sital.

The Indian community of Hong Kong today is very diverse. While many Indians work in traditional businesses like international trade, restaurants, retail and tailoring, thousands are professionals in international companies, finance, insurance, medicine, the media, airlines, shipping, travel agencies, yoga and the diamond business. Indians are multi-lingual. They have their native languages such as Punjabi, Gujarati, Sindhi, Bengali and Tamil though most speak English. In the 2011 census, 37.2 per cent of Indians said they spoke English as their usual language, 4.6 per cent Cantonese and 57.9 per cent another language.

1. Interview with Ray Sital, president of the Council of Hong Kong Indian Association (4/4/2018)

2. Interview with Lal Hardasani, managing director of Lal's Insurance Brokers, and Dr Ravindra Shroff, managing director of Nexus Marine (13/3/2018)

3. "The Overseas Indian Community in Hong Kong" by Professor K.N. Vaid, University of Hong Kong

4. Exhibition description of Tai Kwun (Central Police Station)

Patriarch of the Indian Community

Hari Harilela

→ Hari Harilela, the founder and chairman of the Harilela Group who died in 2014.

The Harilelas are the wealthiest and best known Indian family in Hong Kong. The family business – the Harilela Group – owns and operates 14 hotels in Hong Kong, mainland China, Penang, Singapore, London, Canada and New York. These include the Holiday Inn Golden Mile and Intercontinental Grand Stanford in Kowloon and two Ambassador Hotels at Changi Airport in Singapore. More than 50 members of the family live together in the same giant property in Kowloon Tong; the household staff alone numbers more than 50. There is no comparable family home in Hong Kong – and probably not in the rest of China.

The patriarch of the family, Hari Harilela, died on December 29, 2014, aged 92. He was an important public figure, a close friend to two chief executives of the SAR, an advisor on Hong Kong affairs to the central government in Beijing, and a recipient of numerous awards from the Hong Kong government. He was also a generous philanthropist, donating to charities and tertiary education. He was succeeded as chairman of the Harilela Group by his son, Aron. Hari had five brothers. The family made its first fortune after World War Two in the tailoring

business. In 1959, it established the Harilela Group and went into hotels, which are now its principal business. The group also has export and travel operations.

History

The family has lived in the city since 1911. The first member to come to China was Naroomal Harilela who left his native Sindh province – now in Pakistan – to seek his fortune in Guangzhou. His business did well until the Great Depression. The collapse of the U.S. economy bankrupted his company; he was forced to move with his family to Hong Kong and put his children, including the second son Hari, out to work. Hari decided to become a tailor. It proved to be a very smart decision and brought the family their first fortune. Many other Indians in Hong Kong have followed suit. During World War Two, the Harilelas lived in Hong Kong. The Japanese occupation, from December 1941 to August 1945, was a traumatic period, for them as for other residents of the city. The family members were not interned but fell on hard times; they were able to continue the tailoring business but in a limited way. After the war, the business prospered through sales to soldiers of the British and the American military, in Hong Kong and at bases around Asia. Father Naroomal died in 1948.

In 1959, the brothers established the Harilela Group. In 1961, they went into the hotel business with the acquisition of the Imperial Hotel in Hong Kong. This has become the main business of the group. Its string of 14 hotels stretches across Hong Kong, mainland China, Europe, Canada and the U.S.

Family Home

The family lives in a 40-bedroom mansion on Waterloo Road in Kowloon Tong and an adjoining house with 28 bedrooms. Four generations live together. The house has an underground car park for more than 20 cars, 30 servants, three cooks, six drivers, repairmen and gardeners. The centrepiece is a temple room, which everyone visits daily, before breakfast. Hari had a rich social life, with large parties in a dining hall bedecked with chandeliers; the guests included senior politicians, tycoons and visiting celebrities from India.

Hari was very active in public life and was the best known of the six brothers. He was close friends with two SAR chief executives, Tung Chee-hwa and Donald Tsang Yam-kuen. He was consulted by British colonial governors and post-1997 chief executives alike. He received Hong Kong's Grand Bauhinia Medal and Gold Bauhinia Star and an OBE (Order of the British Empire). "He had a great voice in the government on numerous ethnic minority issues," said Mohan Chugani, president of the Indian Association of Hong Kong. He was an active philanthropist, donating generously to educational institutions, such as the University of Science and Technology. "Charity begins at home. I made my home here, so I will give all the charity to the people of Hong Kong," he said.

He passed away on December 29, 2014, at the age of 92, at his home in Kowloon Tong, with his family at his side. In an announcement, his family described him as a "very dedicated husband, loving father and grandfather, brother, an inspiration to the whole family and a true friend to all." He was succeeded as chairman of the group by his son Aron. "(My father) was generous, humble with an open spirit and a forward mind," said Aron. "He always encouraged me to aspire in all things in life – in learning, in family, in business and also as importantly, with the friends in one's life," he added. "The company remains committed to the values laid down by our founder. As time never stops changing, businesses like ours must be open to new ideas and ways of thinking. In running the Harilela Group, I always remember the lessons my father taught me about the importance of sincerity and honesty in both business and life," he said. Hari was married to his wife Padma for six decades. In addition to his son Aron, Hari also had five daughters.

1.   Harilela Group website

2.   *South China Morning Post* (30/12/2014)

Five Generations of Parsees

Jimmy Minoo Master

→ Jimmy Minoo Master in the Zoroastrian Temple in Causeway Bay.

In the Gloucester Road office of Jimmy Minoo Master, framed photographs of weddings and other family gatherings give a personal touch to the workplace. In one photo, Jimmy can be seen in a long white outfit and black hat, traditional male Parsee attire for weddings and other important occasions. His wife wears a sari that is trimmed with delicate Parsee embroidery.

Jimmy and a partner run a small asset management company – as they have for the past two decades. Born in 1955, Jimmy is the family's fourth generation in Hong Kong. And there is a fifth as represented by his two daughters – one a vet for the SPCA, the other a correspondent for the Thomson Reuters news organisation.

"From what I understand of my family history, my great-grandfather's brother came to Hong Kong and the Canton region around 1910 and worked for Johnson Stokes & Master," he says, referring to one of the oldest law firms in Asia. "After a couple of years, he brought his younger brother to Hong Kong and they decided to establish a trading business here.

"At that time there was a great demand from the Chinese for things like cotton yarn and all sorts of other imports which they used to bring in from India. And then they used to export from China a lot of things like silks and spices and saris to India. "

In the early years of British colonial Hong Kong, the small Parsee community was largely men. Jimmy's grandmother was only the third woman in the community, when she joined her husband as a young bride from India in the 1920s.

"At that time, most of the men came out on their own. They stayed out in Asia for a couple of years and then went back once every two or three years to see their families, see their wives, and perhaps procreate more children," says Jimmy. "But from the 1920s onwards, it became more and more the custom that ladies were brought out from India and slowly you began to see the formation of a complete family-oriented Parsee community in Hong Kong. And that has continued right up until this day."

Jimmy's mother, 92, was born in Hong Kong. Her side of the family was from Mumbai, his father's from Darjeeling. The Parsees are descendants of refugees who left Iran about 1200 years ago and settled along the coastline of Gujarat, India's westernmost state.

"So we have taken on the Gujarati language, we have taken on the Gujarati dress, which is a sari, and many aspects of our life are obviously drawn from Hindu culture and Hindu tradition," says Jimmy. However, having been born and raised here, "I'm more of a Hong Kong boy than anything else."

Parsee children take the name of the father as their middle name. Minoo was Jimmy's father, so that became Jimmy's middle name. Jimmy's daughters both carry the middle name Jimmy. They find it a little unusual having a man's middle name, but Jimmy was eager for the custom to be continued. In pre-colonial days, he says, male Parsees would have been known as "the son of" – so, for example, Jimmy, would have been known as Jimmy, the son of Minoo. But that practice disappeared when the British began codifying the names of Indians for census purposes.

"So you were given a name, either from the place that you came from or from your profession," says Jimmy. "So I would imagine our ancestors somewhere back in time were either schoolteachers or people who were instructive in an educational environment and that's how the name Master must have come about. But if you look within our own Parsee community you will see many trade names, you will see names of places where people have come from, and this practice has continued."

In recent years, Hong Kong's Parsee population has expanded slightly. For years, the small community numbered only about 120-150 people, but more recently it has grown to around 240. This is because "a number of primarily young Parsee families have been sent out from India to work either in the banking and finance industry, or in the logistics industry", he says.

Jimmy praises the secure environment Hong Kong provides for his family. And considering how crowded the city is, he is similarly grateful for policies that allowed Parsees to obtain land for their own cemetery, which dates back to the 1850s.

At the same time, he notes a sense of sadness over the loss of one of the traditional skills once found in this region – the beautiful embroidery work that was used to decorate saris. This delicate and intricate hand embroidery was done in Hong Kong and southern China, and then exported to India.

"That was a huge business for many people. And that skill has been lost. Today in many Parsee households, it's a point of pride to unearth these old sari borders and put them on to saris today and wear them for formal occasions."

The trading company set up by Jimmy's great-grandfather was KS Pavri and Sons Ltd. The business was located on Wyndham Street – the warehouse at street level, offices on the first floor and living quarters on the second. That was where Jimmy grew up.

Many of the documents and memorabilia from that era were lost when the company's godowns were ransacked during the Japanese military occupation of Hong Kong. His family shared space with neighbours in the building in those difficult times. They managed to survive by selling off some of their jewellery for food.

On the floor of Jimmy's office are Iranian carpets. His wife is an Iranian Zoroastrian. "So there is an Iranian aspect to our culture as well. She tries to bring a little bit of that into our daily lives. Her name is Niloufer – which means water lily and we met in Bombay."

"Zoroastrian should not be confused with Parsee. Zoroastrianism refers to the faith. And the Parsees are the descendants of those refugees who left Iran some 1,200 years ago and settled in India. In Iran you would have an Iranian Zoroastrian, whereas in India you would have a Parsee who follows the Zoroastrian faith. So it's important not to mix the two up."

Both of their daughters have married outside the community, one to a Dutchman, the other to an Englishman. "As far as traditions are concerned, I think they feel very Parsee in their outlook," he says of his daughters. "I think we brought them up to understand where and what they are and hopefully they will continue some of the traditions they have seen us perform in the last several decades."

Equality for all HongKongers

Shalini Mahtani & Ravi Gidumal

→ Shalini Mahtani and her husband Ravi Gidumal.

Shalini Mahtani, MBE, and her husband, businessman Ravi Gidumal, have played a major role in the campaign for equal rights for South Asians in Hong Kong. Over the past 25 years they have worked tirelessly for equal rights for Indians, Pakistanis and other minorities to create a society with diversity at its core. They have sought a role for these groups on government committees, company boards and numerous other aspects of local community affairs.

Their list of achievements include Mr Gidumal's successful effort to ensure stateless people from non-ethnic Chinese backgrounds were provided with British passports at the time of Hong Kong's handover to China in 1997. He also teamed up with social worker and fellow activist Fermi Wong in a quest for an anti-discrimination law in the territory. They ultimately reached their goal in 2006.

Following a career in finance, Ms Mahtani founded the NGO Community Business to increase diversity of all kinds. This was followed several years later by the creation of The Zubin Foundation, a leading social policy think tank and charity, named after their son Zubin Mahtani Gidumal, who died suddenly at the age of three in 2009.

Zubin means "to honour or serve", and the organisation bearing his name seeks to fight barriers to fairness and opportunity, advise the government on policies and create empowerment projects.

Born in Hong Kong in 1972, Ms Mahtani is the granddaughter of the late businessman George Harilela, the older brother of Hari Harilela.
"My mum, Mira Harilela, who later became Mira Mahtani, was born in Hong Kong. And my father, Ramesh Mahtani, was born in Hyderabad in Sindh and came here as a young boy," she says. "For my generation what was unique about my parents was that they fell in love. And the big issue at that time was that he was a Hong Kong boy and she was a Kowloon girl. And the Hong Kong-Kowloon divide was enormous. When we think about that today, it's really quite funny."

Turning to her background, she says, "I am, I suppose, one of the older grandchildren of the Harilela family. But being a girl and being a boy is very different. And being a child of a daughter is also very different, because I don't carry the family name. So in our tradition, which I've got to admit I think is wrong, the name goes through the

→ Shalini Mahtani and Ravi Gidumal with their children Anya, left, and Zubin. Zubin died at the age of three. His parents named the Zubin Foundation after him.

boy and traditionally everything in terms of benefit and how you are viewed all goes through the boy.

"The general feeling is that my mum, as the first Harilela born of her generation, she would be married and she would go into another family. So she would no longer be a Harilela. You lose your identity as a woman; you then take on another identity.You belong to another family."

And this continues today. Ms Mahtani reckons she is one of a very few women of Sindhi origin who she knows to have retained her maiden name.
"But I think it's a big ask if families that come from very conservative cultures choose to bring up their children in more liberal cultures and then expect their children to adopt the more conservative values. I do think the Sindhi family structure is very patriarchal, I married a man who was very liberal. We fell in love and his family have been in Hong Kong a long time.

"His father grew up in Shanghai and had been out of India a generation longer than my family. His mum was a working woman and educated. For me, born in

1972, I went to university in 1990 and both from the Harilela side, which is my maternal side, and the Mahtani, which is my paternal side, it was a very big thing. And something I fought for many years to get."

Ms Mahtani recalls an incident at Island School when she was 13. During a history lesson, she was asked about her aspirations and said she would be prime minister of India. "He (the teacher) laughed and said: 'No, Sindhi girls just get married'."

Other forms of discrimination contributed to the couple's zeal in the quest for equality. The man later to become Ms Mahtani's husband, Ravi Gidumal, was out with friends in early 1993 and about to enter a bar in Lan Kwai Fong. His other friends had gone in ahead of him, but he was stopped at the door, and told it was a private party. While he had been aware of the issue of discrimination in Hong Kong, he had never been directly affected by it. He was appalled to discover that racial discrimination was not illegal at that time in Hong Kong. That incident prompted him to take action. He would go on to lead The Indian Resources Group in its campaign for Hong Kong's stateless citizens ahead of the handover and in a fight to ensure they had British citizenship after the handover. He also would work for years with social worker Fermi Wong in the lengthy effort to pass anti-discrimination legislation.

"I grew up with a real mix of friends so while I knew of racism and discrimination as a concept, I didn't appreciate how ingrained it was. To his great credit, my father had bridged the racial divide. Back in the 1950s, he was a member of the Hong Kong Golf Club as an ethnic Indian, which was a big deal," says Mr Gidumal.

But Mr Gidumal's incident in 1993 changed things for him. He and a friend made a real noise about it, involved the media, wrote to then-governor David Wilson, told the Legislative Council and lobbied the government to make racial discrimination illegal. Because of that publicity, a group concerned about the impending statelessness of minorities at the time of the handover contacted Mr Gidumal. These were not just of South Asian heritage, but also included Russians and people from the Middle East.

Mr Gidumal ultimately led a five-year battle, which went from Hong Kong to the House of Lords in London. It resulted in the passage of the British Nationality (Hong Kong) Act 1997 in February of that same year, providing British citizenship to the non-ethnic-Chinese minorities of Hong Kong. This was the first piece of legislation passed in the UK for more than 100 years that started in the House of Lords and then was passed into law by the House of Commons. The group's efforts were supported in the UK by former Hong Kong governors Sir David Wilson and Sir Murray MacLehose.

"A few of us beat a government, that's basically what we did. A bunch of young people went out and changed history in a way and we changed the opportunities for life of many people in Hong Kong. So it was huge."

In 2003, Ms Mahtani set up Community Business, an NGO harnessing the power of business to drive change. This has been done through research, surveys, diversity lists, mentoring, and empowering employees to ensure diversity and inclusion in the workplace. Meanwhile, Mr Gidumal continued his work campaigning for rights for minorities. This included continued efforts with social worker Fermi Wong who was instrumental in bringing about Hong Kong's Race Discrimination Ordinance in 2006.

"I have the ultimate respect for Fermi and what she has done," says Mr Gidumal, "Dedicating most of her life not just to the issue of legislation but addressing the plight of ethnic minorities in Hong Kong". He says his work isn't finished yet and there is a need for more public education.

As for The Zubin Foundation he says: "A lot of the work that the foundation does revolves around ethnic minorities in Hong Kong." "We're a relatively new charity, but Shalini has been working on issues of this nature for a long, long time," he says. "That's really where her passion and her heart is. And the work of her team at the foundation today revolves around issues from special needs education for minorities, to just the general status of minorities in Hong Kong, trying to provide mentorship programmes for them, to give them a lift."

1.   Interview with Ms Shalini Mahtani (26/4/2018)

        Interview with Mr Ravi Gidumal (11/5/2018)
2.

Hong Kong's Bilingual Stand-up Comedian

Vivek Mahbubani

→ Vivek Mahbubani has won Hong Kong's top prize for comedy in both English and Cantonese.

Indian Hongkonger Vivek Mahbubani has just been to St Paul's Co-educational College on MacDonnell Road, their morning assembly guest speaker for their "Stress Relief Week". The schoolchildren will have had a good laugh before starting their lessons, and Vivek, 35, may be inspiring the next generation of stand-up comedians here.

Vivek is bilingual – he grew up speaking English with his Sindhi family in Sai Ying Pun, and he went to local schools learning to not only speak Cantonese but also read and write Chinese to Primary 6. "I can read a menu, and also see when there's an offer with 10 per cent off!" he says.

In his remarkable stand-up career, in 2007 he was crowned Chinese and in 2008 English Funniest Comedian in Hong Kong and was the host of the RTHK television series "Hong Kong Stories". He's also a headliner for the TakeOut Comedy Club Hong Kong.

He also runs his own web-design company, but his stand-up career has taken off to such an extent with gigs across Asia, that he is now solely focusing on that. He's just returned from the Melbourne Comedy Festival where he did a string of shows in Cantonese.

"I would say a good stand-up comedian is able to observe life from a different angle. So the idea is not to live a funnier life, not to see life from a funny angle, but to say "Hey wait a second, never thought of it that way. And then presenting it in a funny way. That's the idea," he says.

He's a third generation Hongkonger. "My grandfather and my father were in the typical Indian import export business, doing whatever made money, selling this, selling that."

"So from what they've told me, my father's side is from Calcutta and my mother's side is from Mumbai. So it's that kind of mix. But they left so long ago that their roots are more than anything in Hong Kong. So a lot came here for business, like one big family and the joke in Hong Kong is that all the Indians know one another."

His parents had an arranged marriage and were keen for their children to learn Cantonese, which has ensured that Vivek is bilingual.

"So this is the twist. I'm Indian. I grew up in Hong Kong, I speak Cantonese and English. My Hindi and Sindhi, which is my own language, are not that good. I can understand it, I know when people are yelling at me. But otherwise if I were in India, I would have to struggle.

"My parents decided that since I was growing up in Hong Kong it was very important for me to learn the local language so they sent me to a Chinese school. Now the challenge was that back then there wasn't much integration of non-Chinese kids in local schools but because of that I was treated just like the next kid – they wouldn't give me special treatment. That helped me to really integrate with society, learn Chinese like anyone else. Learn to read and write and stuff like that."

Vivek says that when he goes to India, "yes, I do feel a sense of belonging there, I do understand why I do things a certain way and I blend in. But I myself thrive on and like the idea that I stick out that I don't fit in – it gives me a whole different perspective on life. So I joke a lot in Hong Kong, that depending on what the situation is I can be the local or I can be the foreigner."

The TakeOut Comedy Club Hong Kong is a perfect platform to hone new skills, he says, for budding comedic performers, but they focus mainly on English shows. So Vivek is producing Cantonese shows. "Our group is called Hall of Laughs. We perform regularly in Hong Kong and find venues. I want kids [who come along to shows] to be able to feel, hey I've got something funny to say, I could try that."

Vivek has an older sister, Krishnaa, 38, who is a chemical engineer with a PhD. "So me and my sister are opposites in that she's academic and I'm more creative. And she's more into the sciences, I'm more into the arts."

Vivek's parents put the emphasis on education when he was growing up, so sometimes they would sacrifice holidays in order to go on study courses in Hong Kong. His parents' marriage was arranged. "Arranged marriages are very common in Indian culture," he says. "Not because we can't be bothered to find someone for ourselves, more like it's just an understanding where we're trying to get to know the family and see if we're all compatible. And some people say there's no love in it. But love can develop as you get along over time, instead of worrying

→ Vivek eyes up a bottle of whisky in Serendib restaurant in Sheung Wan.

about I love her or him but I don't like the parents, where it causes a lot of tension in the family.

"So arranged marriages are a very normal thing. Where the parents at a certain age say okay son, okay daughter, I think it's time you got married, let's go out looking and everything. And we talk to friends, hey do you have anyone who's single, who's interested? Let's get them to meet, let them talk. And it's a very normal thing, you'll meet one, two, or three, and it's like speed dating but with the potential of being married – now!

"My mother's family was very conservative, she was the middle child of five siblings, and so after the two older kids got married, it was her turn."

Vivek regards himself as an Indian Hongkonger.

"I don't like the term ethnic minority because it automatically categorises people. And it's a very grey area, let's be honest. When people think of ethnic minority they think of brown skin. Whereas if I see a Caucasian friend of mine – is he an ethnic minority? Not really. Why? Technically he's still an ethnic minority."

When Vivek goes to give talks to schoolchildren at their morning assembly he points out to them that many iconic aspects that are regarded as the real Hong Kong – the Star Ferry, the University of Hong Kong - were built and funded by a whole mix of people.

"The term ethnic minority makes it sound like there's a group of these people with us. No, we're all Hongkongers, you just happen to be Hong Kong Chinese, and I happen to be Hong Kong Indian. So, yeah, I definitely feel that the term needs to be updated and I believe that it will be updated very soon."

As a boy, Vivek would go with his family every Sunday to the temple. He feels this kind of discipline and time spent with the family is important.

"Sunday is family day, learn your values. But nowadays, I haven't been to that temple in a long time. Nor do my parents tell me to."

Their focus, he says, was on his education. "It wasn't to make me religious but to be a good person."

The
Muslims
of
Hong
Kong

The Muslims of Hong Kong

Hong Kong is home to about 300,000 Muslims, triple the number in 2006. Indonesians account for roughly half of the total, and most are domestic helpers, or maids. Another 40,000 are ethnic Chinese, some 30,000 are from Pakistan while the others are from the Middle East, Africa and Asia, including India. There are about 12,000 local Muslim families – those of mixed South Asian and Chinese ancestry. They are descendants of early Muslim immigrants who married local Chinese women and brought their children up in the Muslim faith. In 2016, Muslims accounted for 4.1 per cent of the city's population, up from 1.3 per cent in 2006.

Indian Muslims have a particularly long connection with Hong Kong as they were among the first soldiers of the British Indian army to arrive on the island. Others worked aboard the cargo ships bringing opium from India. The first British ships to sail into Chinese waters

→ Muslims pray at the Kowloon Mosque & Islamic Centre.

were those of the East India Company, plying the sea routes between Calcutta and ports in Asia as far off as Japan. Those seafarers registered for service in Bombay and Calcutta. The first opium clipper, the "Red River", was built by the British company Jardine Matheson in Calcutta in 1829. Some of those mariners settled in Hong Kong and lived together in the Lower Lascar Row in Central, also known as Moro Kai (street of the people of the Moors). It was in that street that they held their first religious services. Later the Muslim families moved out of the area and Chinese traders moved in, selling curios, old scrolls and relics. The district is now better known as "Cat Street" an oblique reference to how some of those antiques

Chapter 2 —— The Muslims of Hong Kong

were obtained and later sold. Other Indian Muslims, mainly from the Punjab, came to Hong Kong as soldiers in the British Indian Army. Such a career offered a good alternative to the rural poverty into which they were born. After completing their service, they could stay in Hong Kong or use their savings to go home, buy land and build a house, and start a family.

The first mosque in Hong Kong was Jamia Masjid, built in 1850 at 30 Shelley Street in Central. Together with the soldiers and seamen, Indian Muslim businessmen were among the first to make their fortune here, most of them in the business of trading gems and jewellery. They applied to the government to build a mosque. Minutes of the Executive Council meeting on October 25, 1844 recorded the application. In December 1850, the government leased

→ A muslim enters the Jamia Masjid for the 1 o'clock prayer.

a 46,860 square foot plot of land for 999 years and the mosque was built on the site. That same year the Islamic Community Fund was established, with four trustees. The mosque was used for more than 50 years; then, in 1915, it was demolished and a larger one constructed, with room for more than 400 worshippers. It was entirely funded by Haji Mohamed Essack Elias of the Memon Community in Bombay. The mosque is still standing today. It is 70 feet long, 40 feet wide and 20 feet high, with a minaret above. In May 2010, the Hong Kong SAR government listed it as a Grade 1 historical building. It provided money to carry out major repairs and renovation work over the next three years. During the early years of the colony, this mosque served the needs of the Muslim mariners, traders and the 400 who worked as guards in Victoria Prison nearby. According to government records, the first Muslim burial in Hong Kong was in 1828, in a cemetery in Happy Valley. In July 1870, the government allocated a site there as a Muslim cemetery, and the local community built a small mosque nearby. The site was enlarged in 1938. It remains today and includes the tombs of six people killed during World War One and 19 from World War Two. As the British hold over Hong Kong was strengthened, more Indian Muslims moved here, mostly from Punjab. They worked in the police force and prisons, guarded the docks and served as watchmen, bank clerks, ferry supervisors, and government drivers and servants. Diamond traders from South India, especially Muslims, came in large numbers, and the Muslim community grew. Socially, they attained an intermediary status between the British rulers and the local Chinese residents.

→ Islamic Centre in Kowloon

In Kowloon, the first Muslim place of worship was for soldiers of the British Army. At their request, the army granted them a temporary site inside the Whitfield Army Barracks between Austin and Nathan Roads. The first mosque on the Kowloon side of the harbour was built in 1896 on 1,500-square-metre site on Nathan Road for use by the Muslims in the British Army. They had arrived in May 1892 and were accommodated at the Whitfield Barracks nearby. Money

→ (Top) The Muslim Cemetery at Happy Valley.

→ (Bottom) The Muslim Cemetery in Happy
   Valley has gravestones that date back to the 19th
   Century.

for the mosque's construction came from the Muslim soldiers themselves. The mosque was repaired and repainted in 1902. A large concrete pool was installed to store water for the daily ablutions of worshippers. Plants and goldfish were added to help keep the water clean.

The site included accommodation for an imam. Maulvi Gulab Shah was the first imam at the mosque, hailing from Attock, then known as Campbellpur, in the northern Punjab. The mosque also had a guest house for travellers. This support from the colonial government enabled Muslim soldiers to fulfill their religious duties and retain their faith while they served the British empire.

The mosque remained a place of worship for Muslims for over 80 years. But in 1976, construction work for a Mass Transit Railway station nearby caused extensive damage to the building. The Public Works Department declared the structure too dangerous for use. The Incorporated Trustees of the Islamic Community Fund of Hong Kong applied for permission to build a new mosque, and the government approved the proposal in December 1977. In January 1980, the old mosque was demolished and construction of a new one began in March 1981. In 1984, the Hong Kong government rezoned the area and built Kowloon Park alongside it.

The Kowloon Mosque and Islamic Centre, built at a cost of HK$25 million, opened for daily prayers on May 11, 1984. With three floors and a mezzanine, it can accommodate 3,500 worshippers. As at other mosques around the world, prayers are held five times a day – the first at about 5:30 am and the last at about 8:30 pm. Funds for construction were raised from the local Muslim community, with substantial contributions from the Middle East. A plaque at the entrance lists the donors, and they include Chinese Muslims in Hong Kong, Emirates National Bank, the Government of Iraq, the Islamic Solidarity Fund of Jeddah, the National Bank of Pakistan, the Royal Saudi government, the National Commercial Bank of Jeddah and Oman International Finance Limited. The Islamic Community Fund also received compensation from the Mass Transit Railway for its former mosque.

→ An aerial view of the Kowloon Mosque and Islamic Centre inside Kowloon Park.

The new mosque is in the Tsim Sha Tsui district where many Muslims from South Asia live. It was designed by architect I.M. Kadri of Mumbai, in a traditional mosque style that ensures it stands out from the steel and concrete skyscrapers around it. It has four 11-metre-high minarets made of white marble at the corners of the upper terrace and uses white marble on the paving and façade. The main prayer hall can accommodate 1,000 people; there are two smaller halls, with prayers five times a day. Sermons are given in Urdu, English and Arabic, as well as in Cantonese. At the top is a dome five metres in diameter and nine metres high. The mosque attracts nearly one million visitors every year.

The building houses three prayer halls, a library, a kitchen and community hall, separate madrassas for boys and girls and separate ablution areas for men and women. The community hall is used for a variety of purposes, including meetings, educational courses, lectures, prayers and marriage ceremonies. During the important month of Ramadan, this space is converted into a large dining hall to feed over 2,000 Muslims daily free of charge; the cost is covered by the local Muslim community and the event managed by volunteers at the mosque. Ramadan is in the ninth month of the Islamic calendar and during this month, Muslims must fast from dawn until sunset. They must not consume food or liquids, smoke or engage in sexual relations. They must also refrain from sinful behaviour that might negate the rewards of fasting. Ramadan is the busiest month of the year for the mosque. There are daily lectures on the understanding of worship after midday prayers and short talks on character-building and behaviour before breaking the fast at about 6:30 to 7:00 pm each day. At about 9:00 pm each day, the imams recite one-thirtieth of the Quran, to an audience of more than 1,500 people. By the end of Ramadan, they will have recited the entire scripture.

In 2004 and 2005, the centre was renovated at a cost of HK$14 million. The facilities were extended to include a library, a conference room, a management office, two offices for imams and a large kitchen. The library contains more than 4,000 books, in Arabic, English, Urdu and Chinese. Some books introducing Islam are distributed free of charge to Muslims and non-Muslims alike. The washing area on the mezzanine floor was converted into two new madrassas for girls and boys; they are centrally air conditioned and can accommodate more than 200 students. The students learn the Quran in Arabic from qualified teachers. Over 260 children attend daily Quran classes; over 1,000 children at the centre have learnt the entire holy book by heart – thus earning the title of 'hafiz'. The centre also holds courses on Islam for non-Muslims and has a committee responsible for proselytising.

Mufti Muhammad Arshad has been chief imam of Hong Kong since 2001. "We have 16 staff working in the mosque, including four imams," he said in an interview. "Two come from Pakistan, one from India and one is Chinese. We have two classes, with about 300 children per day who learn the Quran. The teachers explain the text and its meaning. We have three-month courses, in English and Chinese, for non-Muslims. We welcome local visitors to visit the mosque. And we have a programme of tours of the mosque for students, during which we answer their questions. We support the needy people and the victims of natural and other disasters, such as the Syrians and the Rohingyas, out of collected donations. We have a Centre of Muslim marriage here; the Immigration Department has authorised me to issue marriage certificates. We also issue certificates for halal food and have library with Islamic books.

"Each day about 2,000 people come here for prayers. We have prayers five times a day and each time we have 500-700 people. It is one of the most actively used mosques in Southeast Asia. It is unique and different to the high-rise buildings around it. It is both a historic and a religious building. It is a combination of tradition, religion and culture. Its dome and minaret show its Islamic culture and its hall demonstrates the religious significance. A minaret is the reflection of history and culture. When people see it from a distance, they recognise it as a place of worship. In earlier times, before the invention of public address systems, minarets were used as a point to call the faithful to prayer. Having four minarets and one dome indicates a mosque as well as the five pillars of Islam," he says.

→ Muslims pray inside the Kowloon Mosque and Islamic Centre.

The mosque is open from dawn until late in the evening. The largest number of worshippers come during the holy month of Ramadan and Eid, which marks the end of Ramadan, when 5,000 people attend. During Ramadan, Radio Television Hong Kong broadcasts a 30-minute programme, during which imams and scholars explain the meaning of the Quran. It is the only registered place in Hong Kong where Muslims can marry; the imam performs the ceremony at the mosque and issues a marriage certificate that is recognised by the government. Like the other mosques, it also serves as a social centre for the Muslim community.

"When Muslims live anywhere, they build a mosque," says the imam. "If not, there is no clue that they lived there. If we see a mosque, it

Chapter 2 —— The Muslims of Hong Kong

→ (Top) Pages of the Quran at Kowloon Mosque and Islamic Centre.

→ (Bottom) A Muslim prays at the Jamia Masjid.

tells us that Muslims lived there. This is the milestone of Muslim history in Hong Kong. It was a gift by the British to the Muslim community. They planted the seeds of people of the (Indian) sub-continent in Hong Kong. They gave it freedom of religion and of expression and a multi-faith society."

It is a prime site, one of the most expensive areas in the territory, in the Tsim Sha Tsui district that is home to hundreds of shops, hotels, restaurants and office buildings. The worshippers include Muslims from India, Pakistan, Bangladesh and Sri Lanka as well as local Chinese and Indonesians, among others. A landmark in Tsim Sha Tsui, it is the largest symbol of Islam in Hong Kong.

→ *Mosque in Happy Valley*

On Hong Kong island, the biggest Muslim place of worship is the Masjid Ammar and Osman Ramju Sadick Islamic Centre on Oi Kwan Road in the Wan Chai. In December 1978, the government appropriated the land on which the Happy Valley mosque stood, to construct approach roads for the Aberdeen Tunnel. As compensation, it provided the community with land on 40 Oi Kwan Road and HK$2.5 million for the building of a new mosque. An eight-storey building was opened on September 14, 1981, with additional funds

→ Muslims pray at the Masjid Ammar and Osman Ramju Sadick Islamic Centre in Wan Chai.

provided by the Islamic Union of Hong Kong. A large part of the funds came from the will of Osman Ramju Sadick, an architect for whom the building is named.

The building contains prayer halls for men and women and washing facilities as well as classrooms, an Islamic canteen, a library, offices for the imam, teachers of the Quran and Islamic organisations, conference and seminar rooms and a medical clinic. On the ground floor, there is a Muslim community kindergarten. The centre can accommodate more than 1,500 people. In the canteen, the many faces of Islam in Hong Kong are clearly visible as worshippers include Chinese, South Asians, Malays, Indonesians, Arabs and Africans. As Indonesian maids are the biggest single group of Muslims in Hong Kong, the Wan Chai mosque sets aside space for them on Sundays, their day off. Programs are offered in Bahasa Indonesia, their national language.

The imam of the mosque is Utham Yang, a native of Shandong in north China. He grew up in a Muslim family, and after graduating from the Beijing Islamic Institute, he went to the Pakistan International Islamic University in Islamabad for further study. He became fluent in Urdu and Arabic in addition to Mandarin. When the mosque was looking for an imam, his knowledge of Chinese Muslim culture as well as that of Pakistan made him a very suitable candidate for a city with Muslim communities from many different backgrounds. Since taking up his post, he has also learnt Cantonese.

There are two other mosques in the city. One is in Stanley, one of the most expensive residential districts on the south side of Hong

→ Utham Yang, Imam of Masjid Ammar and the Osman Ramju Sadick Islamic Centre.

Kong Island. In the 1930s, a prison was built there; Muslim guards moved to that part of the island to work in the prison. They were given a piece of land to offer their daily prayers, and they applied for permission to build a new mosque. This opened on January 1, 1937 on 53 Tung Tau Wan Road inside the prison area; it has a prayer hall, veranda and courtyard. The funds came from the guards themselves. On Fridays, Muslims who do not work in the prison are allowed to worship there. The other mosque is at the Chai Wan Muslim cemetery in Cape Collinson that was established in 1963; prayers are also offered five times a day. Each mosque has classes to instruct young people in the Quran; teachers instruct students to recite and memorise the text, studying Arabic as well as translations of the holy scriptures in their own languages.

→ *Islamic Community Fund*

The five mosques and two cemeteries are owned and managed by the Incorporated Trustees of the Islamic Community Fund of Hong Kong. It was officially registered by the Supreme Court of the colony in September 1850. Nearly two centuries later, it remains the main representative of the community here; it is recognised by the SAR government, which consults it on matters relating to the Muslim community. It organises interfaith dialogue and the proselytising of Islam, issues certification for halal food to suppliers and manufacturers in Hong Kong and mainland China, makes arrangements for major festivals and provides Islamic education.

Social welfare is an obligation of Islam. The Board of Trustees of the ICF operates two funds, Zakat and Sadaqa, through which they provide financial assistance to needy people, including those in prison and victims of natural disasters. With approval of the Correctional Services Department, the board also arranges visits by imams to prisons to meet Muslim inmates and provide religious guidance and joint prayers as well as the observance of requirements of fasting. Hajj, the pilgrimage to Mecca, is one of the five basic pillars of Islam. The Board of Trustees has a committee which organises group of Muslims from Hong Kong to make the trip each

→ Ishaq Ma teaches Islam to students of the ISF Academy at the Masjid Ammar and Osman Ramju Sadick Islamic Centre in Wan Chai.

year. Before they leave, they attend a training course to familiarise with the religious requirements of the pilgrimage.

→ *Social Harmony*

Unlike many cities in the world, Hong Kong is blessed with religious and communal harmony. It remains untouched by the wave of Islamic fundamentalism and violent retaliation by the West that have blighted many countries for the last 20 years. This is the message of Qamar Zaman Minhas, chairman of The Incorporated Trustees of the Islamic Community Fund of Hong Kong in a book published by the Fund, called "Muslim Community Hong Kong". "Hong Kong is a multicultural city with a multiracial population living in peace and harmony. Tolerance for the customs and traditions of all religions and ethnic groups is the beauty of the city's cosmopolitan philosophy and the key factor in its continued success. An estimated 300,000 Muslims live in the heart of the 7.5 million population of Hong Kong. The Board of Trustees has managed to create a suitable environment for these diverse groups of Muslims to live together in peace and harmony. Due to recent changes in global politics, the present times are tough and obviously there is a huge demand to come together and stay united for the peaceful co-existence of different communities."

The book goes on to say: "Hong Kong is a multi-lingual, multi-cultural and multi-religious city. The secret of its success and beauty lives in its highly diversified environment where people belonging to different faiths have full freedom and liberty to live their daily lives and practise the religion of their choice. The mutual understanding and co-operation present among the people is the key to the city's peace and prosperity. Kowloon Mosque has joined hands with the interfaith network of Hong Kong and organised interfaith meetings in the mosque on many occasions. For three years, Hong Kong University has been organising interfaith dialogues in which Muslim, Christian and Jewish scholars participate actively. Chief Imam Mufti Muhammad Arshad represented the community of Hong Kong on two occasions ... We thank the SAR Government for maintaining a close and friendly relationship with the Muslim community and allowing us the freedom and liberty to practise our religion. For the last 175 years, Muslims have been living peacefully in Hong Kong. We are also grateful to the government for providing two pieces of land for new Islamic centres."

As a place to live, Hong Kong offers many benefits to Muslims as well as other minority groups. They have freedom to practise their religion and eat according to their dietary rules. They have the freedom to dress as they wish – in a conservative or modern style, with or without a headscarf. In some countries, it is mandatory for women to wear a headscarf; in others, it is forbidden in certain designated places. Muslims may play the sports they wish and arrange their social and recreational life as they wish. Muslim women are free

→ (Top and Bottom) Muslims attend the Eid al-Fitr on 15 June 2018 at Victoria Park. This marks the end of Ramadan.

to choose the education and training they desire. In some Islamic countries, they must stay at home, cannot receive an advanced education and are limited in their life and career choices. Hong Kong is also one of the safest cities in the world and has an excellent public transport system. A Muslim here does not face the threat of being insulted or attacked in public places – unlike in many cities in Europe. There is a shortage of mosques – but this is a result of the sudden increase in the Muslim population, extremely high land prices and the comparative poverty of many believers. It is not due to government or public opposition to the construction of mosques. There is no public debate about the "Islamic threat", as in many places in the West. Hong Kong residents enjoy freedom of worship and its various religious group live together peacefully.

→ *Shortage of Mosques*

The number of mosques in Hong Kong is insufficient to meet demand from the Muslim community. According to a fact sheet "Religious Facilities in Hong Kong", published in December 2017 by the Research Office of the Legislative Council Secretariat, the number of Muslims in the city reached 300,000 in 2016, compared to 90,000 in 2007. But there are only six official mosques serving them, compared to 1,446 Protestant churches and 94 Catholic churches. Of the mosques, four are on Hong Kong Island and two are in Kowloon. There is no mosque in the New Territories, where more than half the Pakistanis and Indonesians lived in 2016. Faced with this shortage, Muslims have turned apartments into places of worship and even construction sites in Yuen Long have been used as makeshift sites for prayer. The main reasons for this are the high cost of land in Hong Kong and the limited income of many members of the Muslim community. Most Muslims in Hong Kong work as domestic maids, security guards or on construction sites, and their income is comparatively limited. Unlike in a number of European countries, there is no public opposition to the building of mosques and there is no public debate on the threat to public safety from "jihadis" fueling anti-Islam sentiment.

→ A Muslim prays at Kam Shan Country Park in Hong Kong.

One requirement of a pious Muslim is to pray five times a day. This is not easy for one who is working in a factory, shop, building site or other establishments not owned by a fellow Muslim. Most Hong Kong firms are not willing to allow staff members to leave their place of work regularly for prayers. The tens of thousands of Indonesians who work as domestic maids face different challenges. According to Hong Kong law, they must live in the apartment of the person employing them and follow the instructions of their employers. Their duties include preparing food for the family. Since pork is the most popular meat in Hong Kong, they will often be instructed to prepare it, even if they do not eat it themselves. Despite their unease in handling this "unclean" food, they must do as they are told. It is also difficult for them to follow all the observances of Islam and the requirement of festivals, when they have many duties to perform every day for their employer.

→ *The Chief Imam*

Mufti Muhammad Arshad is a native of Pakistan who moved to Hong Kong in 2001 at the invitation of the local community. At the time he was serving in the Pakistan Air Force. He speaks Urdu, English, Arabic and Punjabi.

"In 2001, I was in the Pakistani Air Force. I saw this as a good opportunity, a job in which I could make progress. They invited me and I delivered a talk. They gave me a contract for two years, then another two years, and later (made the offer) permanent. I have a Hong Kong passport and permanent residence status. I have four

→ Mufti Muhammad Arshad, Chief Imam, reads the Quran at the Kowloon Mosque and Islamic Centre.

children, aged from 26 to two. They went to schools here and are settled here. We consider Hong Kong as our home. I used to visit Pakistan once or twice a year. When you spend most of your time in one place, it is hard to adjust to another. I sometimes think of going home but my wife vetoes the idea. She is very happy here. Very few Pakistanis who have left return to live there – only those who have a very solid background. In Pakistan, there is no big role for imams as there is here." As the leader of the Muslim community in Hong Kong, he is often called upon to mediate and rule on matters between rival groups or families, with the aim of reconciling family disputes out of court.

He praised the British for their support for Islam in Hong Kong. "There are five permanent mosques in Hong Kong, all on land granted by the British. During the colonial period, the British built mosques in Asia. I have seen them in other countries, such as Malaysia and Singapore. We should thank the British for granting the land for the mosques as well as for the Muslim Cemetery." He said Muslims had made a major contribution to the city. "Before 1997, there was no big project in Hong Kong without them, such as major bridges and the airport. Muslims worked in all sectors of life, as doctors, teachers, engineers, policemen and in the Correctional Services Department.

The imam sees his mission as extending an understanding of Islam into the wider community. "I take part in inter-faith meetings; we participate in local forums on Islam and inter-faith dialogue." These have taken place both at the mosque and Hong Kong University. His mission is to help the city preserve its precious communal harmony from the violent extremism that has blighted many cities around the world. "We have links with people of other faiths, like Jews, Buddhists, Hindus and Christians. There are problems in other countries but we have to leave the problems there and live here in harmony. We must prove that we are people of peace. Hong Kong is a good place, offering freedom of expression and religion. We must do the maximum we can."

He has taken part in a number of public demonstrations, approved by the police. "After September 11 in 2001, I took part in a memorial service for the 9/11 victims organised by the American Chamber of Commerce, with the chief executive of Hong Kong and representatives of AmCham and the U.S. Consulate. The system in Hong Kong is good and it works. We must preserve it. It is good for local people." He has also taken part in peaceful protests against what he considered insults to his religion. One was against the burning of the Quran in the U.S. a few years ago. "In this, we were joined by Christian people also. We had a total of 5,000 people at Chater Garden. It was not against any particular country or people but to show our respect for all holy books and demand respect for the Holy Quran. We also had a protest against the cartoon of the Prophet in Denmark. Yes, sometimes some of our people are angry. It is challenging to keep them calm. We showed that Muslims of Hong Kong in a state of anger remain peaceful. We must not give a bad name to Muslims."

The situation of some Muslims has changed for the worse since the handover, however. "1997 had a big effect on our community. People were afraid. A few thousand left and moved to the UK, the US and Australia. Many used to hold Indian and Pakistani passports; they were able to get full UK passports. They moved to the UK. Those who stayed have to struggle more. Most work in low-paying jobs. Costs are high in Hong Kong and the city is congested and very expensive. It is hard to survive. Many work two to three jobs. The UK is cheaper and life is easier; housing and the basic necessities are covered. If people have the chance, they will go there."

One main reason for the change for the worse was a strict requirement for written and spoken Chinese for posts in the government, a major employer of the Muslim community before 1997. "Between 1997 and 2015, no South Asian joined the Hong Kong police; they did not recruit any because of the Chinese-language requirement," he says.

This is a complicated issue – why do most minorities, including

→ Balancing his load, a worker walks along a street in Kwai Chung.

Muslims, not have a high level of reading and writing Chinese? Is this the responsibility of the city's educational system or the individuals themselves?

"The responsibility for this lies both with the individual person and family and also with the government," the imam says. "The government is more responsible. The government should accept that non-Chinese are part of the system. It should ensure that those going through the school system master the Chinese language. It should compel all schools to teach it. If not, then open jobs to people who do not have a good command of it. If you go to department stores, the MTR (underground rail system) and buses, you see only Chinese staff. Those jobs that do not require proficiency in Chinese should be open to non-Chinese people. There should be space for them."

Chapter 2 —— The Muslims of Hong Kong

→ *Partition*

Historically, the Muslims from India in Hong Kong were not as wealthy or successful as their compatriots, such as the Parsees, Sikhs and Sindhis, who often benefited in trade and commerce with the aid of global business networks. The Partition of British India in 1947 into the independent states of India and Pakistan was a national tragedy. It resulted in the displacement of 14 million people along religious lines and the death of tens of thousands. Some estimates put the number of dead at two million. The inter-communal violence before and during Partition poisoned relations between the two countries. That toxic atmosphere exists to the present day. Most of those displaced had to leave their land, homes and possessions behind and start a new life with little or nothing in a place that was

→ Wired for sound, a man has a sit-down on Ping Fu Path.

unfamiliar to them. The two new states have fought four wars and many border skirmishes. Both sides have developed nuclear weapons out of fear of the other.

Fortunately, however, this conflict has found no echo among the South Asian communities of Hong Kong. There has been no violence among them. "Wars between India and Pakistan have had no impact here," said Imam Yang. The main change was that the Indian Muslims living here had to choose to which of the two states they wished to belong. A majority chose the Muslim state, Pakistan; they and their descendants carry its passport. A minority chose to remain Indian citizens; now there are fewer than 5,000 Indian Muslims in the city, compared to 30,000 Pakistanis. "In the Indian Recreation Club, there are people of all religions," says Imam Yang. "Muslims work in harmony with Hindus and Sikhs. The canteen is halal, out of respect for the Muslims, and the chairman is a Muslim." The club celebrated its 100th anniversary and both communities participated, he said. Founded in 1917, it is located at Caroline Hill Road in Causeway Bay. It is open to people of all nationalities. It offers a wide range of sports facilities, including tennis, lawn bowls, soccer, badminton, hockey and cricket. Its bar and dining room provide Indian and Chinese cuisine and alcoholic and non-alcoholic drinks.

The main impact of Partition on Hong Kong was economic. The severe disruption of the lives of tens of thousands of people persuaded some of them to come here to seek a better life. "After Partition, those who came from Pakistan were mainly labourers and watchmen, not business people. It remained easy to enter Hong Kong until the handover in 1997," said Yang.

→ *Handover*

The city's return to China in 1997 had a major impact on the Muslim community here, as it did on other South Asians. Hong Kong changed from being a British colony into a Chinese city. While English remains an official language, Chinese became the more important language. Some Muslims emigrated to the United States, Australia and elsewhere. Many of those who obtained a full UK passport emigrated there. Very few went to Pakistan. Under the British, the government had been an important employer of Muslims, as policemen, prison officers and in other institutions. But when the post-1997 government introduced a requirement for the civil service of a high level for reading and writing Chinese, a majority of Muslims, like other South Asians, could not meet this standard. As a result, no South Asian joined the Hong Kong police between 1997 and 2015. After the handover, it became difficult for low-skilled people to enter the city. Imam Yang says: "Since the handover, it has become very difficult (for Pakistanis to enter Hong Kong). You need capital and a sponsor. Some arrive illegally, paying thousands of U.S. dollars to snakeheads to be smuggled in from Shenzhen. Because China and Pakistan have close relations, it is easy for a Pakistani to enter China. They go to Guangzhou and Shenzhen and then try to come here." So the Pakistani community is mostly those who were here before 1997 and their descendants. "They are poorer than the Indians," says Imam Yang.

→ *Language*

The challenges of language which a Muslim from South Asia faces in Hong Kong are formidable. At home, he is likely to speak the language of his native place, probably Urdu or Punjabi. At the mosque, he must learn the Quran in its original Arabic. It is a mark of piety to memorise portions of the sacred book; the most honourable is to memorise the entire Quran. The school he attends is likely to use English, so he must master that as well.

But more than 90 per cent of Hong Kong's population speak Cantonese and write Chinese characters. Chinese is the language of government and commerce as well as most instruction in schools. Chinese characters need to be learnt individually; there is no alphabet. The national language of China is Mandarin, which generally uses the same characters as Cantonese, though the two dialects are mutually unintelligible. Mandarin is increasingly used

→ (Top) "Truck Culture", a Pakistani owned truck is covered with traditional decorations.

(Bottom) A cook in the Bismillah Kebab House which serves Halal food inside Chungking
→ Mansions.

in Hong Kong, especially by tourists, business people and migrants from mainland China. For a long-term resident of Hong Kong, Cantonese is the most important means of communication.

How is the young Muslim to adapt to this Tower of Babel? How many hours does he have in the day to learn all these thousands of words and the different scripts used to write them? His personal and social life is likely to be centred around his family and his community. He faces strong family pressure to find a spouse within his community; if not, then at least a Muslim, rather than a non-Muslim. This will push him to remain among his own people and have limited contact with Chinese. Another constraint is diet. An observant Muslim should eat 'halal', that is food prepared according to Islamic regulations, and avoid drinking alcohol. This is no easy matter in Hong Kong. For Chinese in the city, the most important meat is pork, which is forbidden to Muslims. In addition, a Muslim would not eat or drink from a vessel that might have had contact with pork fat or any derivative of the animal. So the only safe places to eat are at home or in restaurants that imams have designated as 'halal'. The number of such restaurants in Hong Kong is limited. One chain popular among Muslims is McDonald's, which offers meals that clearly contain no pork or pork fat.

Another constraint is a limited knowledge of Chinese characters; a person who cannot read a menu may have difficulty deciding what to eat at a restaurant. These dietary regulations have a major impact on a young Muslim who wants to improve his or her knowledge of Chinese people and their language. In Hong Kong, as elsewhere in the world, eating meals together is the most important form of social contact. As one of the culinary paradises of the world, Hong Kong offers an astonishing range of cuisines, available at all hours of the day and night. But an observant Muslim must decline many of these invitations because he or she cannot be sure that the food on the table conforms to halal regulations. These dietary rules and the instruction to abstain from alcohol are major obstacles to forming social relations with Chinese and learning about their language, culture and society.

→ Shreya Gurung from Nepal and Arsy Nur Dinarti from Indonesia talk during their lunch break at the Islamic Kasim Tuet Memorial College.

→ *Education*

The question of where to send their children to school is a complex one for Muslim parents. If they want their children to have an Islamic education, they can choose one of five schools operated by the Chinese Muslim Cultural and Fraternal Association. Founded in 1922, it operates two kindergartens, two primary schools and one middle school. They follow the same curriculum as local schools and add Muslim elements. These include the teaching of Islam, providing halal food and wearing Islamic style uniforms. The problem is that the schools are few, far apart and do not offer a 'through-train' from kindergarten to graduation ahead of university. The other options are mainstream government schools, most of which teach in Cantonese. There also are 48 international schools, which teach in English or

→ (Top) Students concentrate in class at the Islamic
Kasim Tuet Memorial College.

→ (Bottom) Girls enjoy their lunch at the Islamic
Kasim Tuet Memorial College.

another foreign language, but whose fees are far beyond the budget of most Muslim families. There also are more than 30 schools designated by the government for ethnic minority children that use English as the main teaching medium.

On its website, the Hong Kong Education Bureau said that it was committed to assisting all non-Chinese-speaking students (NCS) in adapting to the local education system and integrating into the community as early as possible. "Some NCS students encounter learning difficulties and adjustment problems when they study in local schools. Greater care and help from schools, teachers and parents are required so that these students can adapt to the local education system and integrate into the community quickly. The Hong Kong Education Bureau (EDB) has provided various support services to school administrators, teachers and parents to cater for the common learning and adaptation needs of the NCS students. This information platform provides an electronic channel through which school administrators, teachers, parents and the public caring about the education of NCS students can obtain useful information and related resources more quickly and directly."

The bureau provides financial grants to these schools to help implement these support programmes. About 60 per cent of non-

Chinese-speaking students are studying in these designated schools. Hong Kong government statistics show that only a limited number of ethnic minority children reach university. A report by the Equality Opportunity Commission in 2012 found that ethnic minorities, excluding Caucasians, comprised 3.2 per cent of pre-primary students but only 1.1 per cent of senior secondary students and 0.59 per cent of those at the tertiary education level. According to Unison, a Hong Kong non-governmental organisation founded in 2001 to aid ethnic minorities, only one per cent of non-Chinese-speaking students enter local universities each year, compared to more than 20 per cent of the students from mainstream schools. A key obstacle is the lack of proficiency in written and spoken Chinese. "Many ethnic minorities reflect to us that it is increasingly difficult in Hong Kong to be competitive in the job market and gain opportunities and information if they only know English but not Chinese," says Unison on its website. "Written Chinese and spoken Cantonese are the most commonly used languages in Hong Kong. We think that the government has the responsibility to provide enough opportunities and support to help ethnic minorities become proficient in Chinese, especially in the public education system ... It is better to mix ethnic minority and Chinese students in the same school; this enables ethnic minority students to understand mainstream society better and helps ethnic minority students learn the Chinese language better by providing a better Chinese-speaking environment." For a Muslim parent, then, the best way for their children to learn Chinese is to attend a mainstream local school that uses Cantonese as its main medium of instruction.

This is a complicated issue. The Hong Kong education system is fiercely competitive; many students go abroad for education because they cannot find a place in a local university. To help their children, many Chinese parents hire private tutors to give them extra one-on-one instruction in the evenings and on weekends, especially to prepare them for the many exams. While Chinese children speak Cantonese and write characters at home, Pakistani children use the native tongue of their families. Their parents may be unable to help them in their studies using English, let alone Chinese. Their long

→ Students relax during a lunch break at the Islamic Kasim Tuet Memorial College.

working hours may leave little time or energy to assist their children. A report issued by the government Equal Opportunities Commission in March 2018 found that over 70 per cent of mainstream kindergartens in a survey were totally or mostly inaccessible to NCS parents; they provided information only in Chinese or the legal minimum in English. While the government bans discrimination against NCS students and provides additional funds to kindergartens that admit eight or more of them, many kindergartens do not wish to. It is often seen as additional work and requiring more staff to help them, especially in learning Chinese. Similarly, Chinese parents prefer to send their children to mainstream schools rather than those designated for NCS students. That is the safer option and the one more likely to get their children into university, at home or overseas. The result is that the majority of ethnic minority children are educated in English. While many speak Cantonese, their written

Chinese is not good enough to enter universities that have higher requirements, and they may not be qualified for most government jobs.

Many Hong Kong people say that it is up to the ethnic minorities themselves to improve their language ability. They argue that, when Chinese emigrate to English- or French-speaking countries, they must learn the language of their new country. Hong Kong is full of schools, institutions, teachers and websites that offer classes in Chinese; so ethnic minorities – including Westerners – should take advantage of these classes and not complain about their lack of fluency, they argue.

Official figures released in the 2016 population by-census revealed how much needs to be done to bring those with South Asian heritage to the same level as the Chinese. Ethnic minorities accounted for eight per cent of the total population (3.6 per cent, excluding foreign domestic helpers). The poverty rate among them reached 19.4 per cent, up from 15.8 per cent in 2011. Pakistanis and Nepalis are the poorest. The same survey found that 64.3 per cent of those aged 5-14 were able to read Chinese – although their reading skills were lower than those of their ethnic Chinese peers. Writing in the *South China Morning Post*, Albert Chan, chairperson of the Equal Opportunities Commission, said: "It is imperative that the younger generation get all the support they need to join the workforce on an equal footing. Currently, many ethnic minorities only know the basics of Chinese, which many employers consider inadequate...Chinese language learning for ethnic minorities has to be improved. Right now, the situation is less than satisfactory." On March 11, 2018, the government announced that it would lower its Chinese-language proficiency requirement for 22 categories of government jobs, bringing to 53 the total with requirements reduced since 2010. The latest batch of 22 include programmers, treasury accountants and laboratory attendants. It said that, over the previous six years, 60 people with a South Asian background have become police officers and inspectors.

An exhausted Hong Kong Pakistani student staring at his dictionary of Chinese characters might wonder about the unfairness of it all. Most Caucasians who live in Hong Kong have a very poor understanding of Cantonese. Many who have lived here for decades do not speak a word and cannot write a single character. If they learn

Chinese, it is more likely to be Mandarin, the national language that is spoken all over the country. "Why do I have to learn all this and not the guailaos ?" the student asks, referring to Caucasians. The answer is that most Westerners live in another universe. They work in occupations where Cantonese is not necessarily a requirement. They have a social and recreational life with other Caucasians and Chinese who speak English. But history and destiny have placed many Muslim families in another corner of the Hong Kong world; for them, mastery of Cantonese and Chinese characters is vital for the future.

1. Interview with Imam Uthman Yang (11/4/2018)

2. Interview with Mufti Muhammad Arshad (11/4/2018)

3. "Muslim Community Hong Kong" by the Incorporated Trustees of the Islamic Community Fund of Hong Kong

4. "Islam in Hong Kong", prepared by Mufti Muhammad Arshad, chief imam of Hong Kong

5. Fact sheet "Religious Facilities in Hong Kong", published in December 2017 by the Research Office of the Legislative Council Secretariat

6. "Understanding South Asian Minorities in Hong Kong", by John Nguyet Erni and Lisa Yuk-ming Leung, Hong Kong University Press, 2014

7. "Islam in Hong Kong – Muslims and Everyday Life in China's World City" by Paul O'Connor, Hong Kong University Press, 2012

8. "Beyond the Hassle and Hustle – Stories of Kwai Chung Cross-Cultural Community", HKSKH Lady MacLehose Centre and Services for Ethnic Minorities

9. *South China Morning Post* (20/3/2018)

Hero Who Made the Ultimate Sacrifice

Captain Mateen Ahmed Ansari

→ Caption Ansari's grave is situated at Stanley Military Cemetery.

Captain Mateen Ahmed Ansari was just 26 when he was beheaded on Stanley Beach in 1943 for refusing to renounce his loyalty to Britain and persuade soldiers under his command to pledge support to the Japanese occupation forces in Hong Kong. Despite being an ardent Indian nationalist, Ansari was serving in the British forces when he was taken prisoner by the Japanese. His integrity and endurance earned him a posthumous George Cross medal from the UK.

He was born into a privileged Muslim family in Hyderabad in 1915, the second son of Begum Ansari, the Registrar of Osmania University in Andhra Pradesh. He reportedly survived both the bubonic plague and cholera as a child before going on to university and then training at the Royal Indian Military College in Dehradun.

After enlisting in the British Indian Army, he was then sent for officer training at the Royal Military Academy, Sandhurst in the UK and was given the King's Commission. He came to Hong Kong in late 1940 as part of the 5th Battalion, 7th Rajput Regiment. When Japanese forces invaded Hong Kong on December 8, 1941, Ansari and his troops were positioned on Devil's Peak,

next to Lei Yue Mun, and the members of the regiment held their position for a week before withdrawing from Kowloon to Hong Kong Island. After the British surrender on December 25, 1941, Ansari opted to stay with his men rather than go to an officers' camp. He was also a member of the British Army Aid Group, an organization in southern China which helped British and allied forces escape.

After initially being treated relatively well, the Japanese military subsequently discovered that Ansari was an aristocrat, and tried to pressure him to persuade his soldiers to join Japan's Indian National Army. Despite his nationalist sentiments, Ansari refused. In May 1943, he was incarcerated in Stanley Prison where he was starved and tortured. He was returned to the ordinary prison camp in September 1943 but continued to organize resistance and help his fellow prisoners escape. Once again he was sent to Stanley Prison where his torture resumed. On October 29, 1943, Ansari was taken out of solitary confinement and condemned to death along with more than 30 other Indian, British and Chinese prisoners. He was beheaded on Stanley Beach.

According to the Armed Forces Muslim

→ The Japanese occupying forces search Indian soldiers, who had formed part of the defence of Hong Kong, and were prisoners of war after the British surrender on December 25, 1941.

Association (UK), The Times of India reported in 1945 that some of the 330 rescued Indians on board HM Hospital Ship Oxfordshire, which was used to repatriate the wounded from Hong Kong after the war, praised Captain Ansari calling him "one of the greatest heroes of the prison camps at Hong Kong".

He is buried in Stanley Military Cemetery in a collective grave. In April 1946, he was awarded a posthumous George Cross by Britain's King George VI. In the London Gazette of March 18, 1946, it said Ansari was: "Awarded the George Cross for most conspicuous gallantry in carrying out hazardous work in a very brave manner". His medal is displayed at the Pakistan Army Museum in Rawalpindi, Pakistan.

1.   The Armed Forces Muslim Association (UK)

2.   Peter E. Hamilton Dictionary of Hong Kong Biography. Edited by May Holdsworth and Christopher Munn, Hong Kong University Press, 2012

3.   The Comprehensive Guide to the Victoria and George Cross.

Defender
of Human Rights

Justice Kemal Bokhary

→ Justice Kemal Bokhary in his study at his home in Stanley.

Kemal Bokhary is well known in Hong Kong for his long and distinguished career as a barrister and judge. After Hong Kong's return to China in 1997, he became a permanent judge on the Court of Final Appeal, the highest court for matters of local law.

Born in 1947, he was called to the English Bar in 1970. In the following year, he was admitted to the Hong Kong Bar. He was a junior barrister from 1971 to 1983 and then a Queen's Counsel from 1983 to 1989. In 1989 he was appointed to the High Court, and in 1993 he was elevated to the Court of Appeal. He is one of the founding justices of the Court of Final Appeal, becoming one of its permanent judges on July 1, 1997. On reaching retirement age in 2012, he became a non-permanent judge of that court, a position he continues to hold.

He also edits Hong Kong's authorised law reports as well as a number of textbooks. He is the author of five books and is currently working on his sixth. His wife (formerly Mrs Justice Verina Bokhary of the High Court) retired recently. She returns to the High Court to hear cases for two months a year. Mr Justice Bokhary refers to these activities as their "part-time work". Their "full-time work", he says, is that of being loving grandparents to five grandchildren. After three daughters, they now have five grandsons, and he notes this involves "learning a new set of skills". They consider their grandchildren the centre of their lives.

Married for 41 years, he quotes the concluding paragraph of his memoirs Recollections (published by Sweet & Maxwell in 2013), to describe how he feels about his wife: "She deserves better than the broken promise which she has received from me. Long ago, I promised her that we would grow old together. Well, we are together. And I have certainly grown old. But she is as young and beautiful as they day we met."

His ancestors on his mother's side were traders. They journeyed by sea from the Middle East across the Indian Ocean, through the Straits of Malacca, into the South China Sea and on to Hong Kong. His maternal great-great-grandfather arrived here a decade or so before Hong Kong came under British administration. He married a Chinese lady.

The maiden name of Mr Justice Bokhary's mother is Arculli. Ronald Arculli, the veteran lawyer, who has served on the Legislative Council and Executive Council, is a cousin. Kemal and Verina Bokhary met in Sir Oswald Cheung QC's chambers where they served pupillage with Mr Arculli (who was a barrister before becoming a solicitor).

His ancestors on his father's side settled in Bokhara in Uzbekistan, and the family takes its name from that city. At some point they migrated to Jalalabad in Afghanistan, and took the name Jalali. But when they migrated through the Khyber Pass into the city of Peshawar in the North West Frontier Province of what is now Pakistan, they reverted to the name of Bokhary. "We realized that we couldn't keep changing our name every time we moved."

Mr Justice Bokhary, who has an elder brother and a younger sister, is the second son of Daoud Bokhary, who is now nearly 100 years of age and worked for the Wharf Company for many years before becoming a stockbroker. Mr Daoud Bokhary had served in the British Indian Army and took part in the Burma Campaign before coming to Hong Kong as part of the British liberation forces at the conclusion of World War Two. Here he met Halima Arculli who became his wife. Of his mother, the judge says: "She was a fearless woman who was a human rights activist in Japanese-occupied Hong Kong."

After their marriage, his parents settled in Peshawar for a time. But his mother was extremely close to one of her sisters, Rahima Ismail, and missed her so much that she wanted to return to Hong Kong. "It was then uncertain whether my father would fare well in civilian life in Hong Kong," he says. "But he did as a man should do by giving his wife what she wanted - and things turned out well." As to that sister of his mother's, he says: "She was a wonderful person, who was the greatest influence in my life. Her husband, S.A. Ismail, was the gentlest and kindest man I have ever known.

"When I was growing up and my father was with the Wharf Company," he says. "He was given 'home leave' of six months every four years, and we spent that home leave in Peshawar."

"Being of mixed race, I was in an ethnic minority in Peshawar just as I am in Hong Kong," he says. "As it happens, that has not disadvantaged me. But that

→ Mr Justice Kemal Bokhary at his home in Stanley.

→ Kemal and Verina Bokhary with two of their grandsons.

is far from saying that nobody else is ever disadvantaged by reason of being in an ethnic minority. And generally speaking, people who have overcome challenges must guard against imagining that everybody else can overcome their challenges without help. That is one of the reasons why I feel strongly that there must be full enforcement not only of human rights of a civil and political nature but also those of a socio-economic nature, involving things such as education, housing, medical care and social welfare for those who need it."

He is also a strong believer in democratic government, and the need to work towards that goal in Hong Kong. In seeking to further democracy and human rights, he believes in trying to persuade rather than criticise.

Mr Justice Bokhary, a Muslim, says that he is able to see the good in other religions and philosophies, and is aware that in enforcing Hong Kong's Basic Law, one is enforcing a secular constitution, not what St. Thomas Aquinas called "inward things". While serving as a High Court judge, he conducted the inquiry into a 1993 New Year's stampede in Lan Kwai Fong which resulted in 21 deaths. The judge made recommendations for avoiding such tragic accidents in future.

The cases which he heard in the Court of Final Appeal include the right of abode cases in which how the court interpreted the Basic Law in favour of the abode-seekers was followed by a reinterpretation by the Standing Committee of the National People's Congress. After the reinterpretation it became vitally important, he says, for the court to show it had not been deterred from doing what it believed to be right.

At his "farewell sitting", upon retirement as a permanent judge in 2012, he warned of storm clouds ahead for the rule of law, but he said that he believed the court would be able to stand up in any possible storm.

He is cautiously optimistic about Hong Kong's future. "We have overcome so many difficulties in the past," he says. "We are entitled to believe that we can overcome our present difficulties.

"While it is always possible to point to other places and other times with far greater problems than our present problems, the task is to make Hong Kong the best that it can be," he says.

As a student, he spent a great deal of time watching cases in Lord Denning's court in London. It was, he says, a good way to learn what the law was really about.

Asked about his first case, he said that it was a landlord and tenant case in which his cross-examination of the other side's witness consisted of one question. That may have been why he won that case, he says, as the presiding judge was particularly averse to long-winded legal arguments.

Throughout his career at the Bar, his practice was mainly commercial, almost exclusively so in later years. But in the first few years, about 25 percent of his cases were criminal cases. He also handled a number of personal injury cases. Eventually, practically none of his cases were criminal cases, and he did fewer and fewer personal injury cases. But throughout his career, he would from time to time represent people who had been rendered quadriplegic. He said: "The thing to do was visit them at home, see what they had to cope with, then take them to Rehabaid to select the appropriate appliances. That way, we managed to achieve record awards, and sometimes even secured rehousing for the client at the insurers' expense."

Ahead of the interview, Mr Justice Bokhary had been drawing a map for a treasure hunt for his eldest grandson Zane and Zane's friends. From his study at his house in Stanley, he walked down to a room full of toy spaceships and rockets he had made. He spends a lot of time making toys for his grandchildren, explaining: "They have a lot of very expensive toys, quite a few of them from Verina and me, but it is important that they have some which cost nothing. Those made by me are the ones which most remind them of how much I love them."

Sikhs –
Lions
and
Princesses
from the
Punjab

Sikhs – Lions and Princesses from the Punjab

An important part of the Indian community are the Sikhs. There are 15,000 in Hong Kong, and they trace their origins to the Punjab region of northwest India. At the time of Partition in 1947, Punjab was divided in two, with the western part going to Pakistan and the eastern part to India. Today there are 27 million Sikhs throughout the world, of whom 21 million live in India, though many reside in the United States, Canada, the United Kingdom, Malaysia and Australia.

Sikhism is a religion founded in Punjab at the end of the 15th century. It is based on the spiritual teachings of Guru Nanak Dev Ji, the first guru (1469-1539), and the nine gurus who succeeded him. Appalled by the rigid caste system he found prevalent in the India into which he was born, he established a new religion based on the following four principles – God is One, mankind is equal,

→ Sikhs in the Hong Kong Police around 1892-1910.

irrespective of caste, creed and religion; no discrimination against women; freedom of religion and no forced conversion; and universal brotherhood. Sikhs may not smoke or drink alcohol. They may not cut hair from any part of their body, because hair is a gift of God. It should be combed twice daily, tied in place and covered by a turban. This makes a Sikh man easy to recognise. Sikh men have the word "Singh" (lion) as their middle or last name; Sikh women have the word "Kaur" (princess) as their middle or last name. The guru chose these names as signs of equality and to raise the status of women. The geographic and spiritual centre of the religion is the Golden Temple, set in the middle of a lake in Amritsar, in the Punjab.

→ A Sikh and a Chinese police officer in Hong Kong, early 20th century.

After the British conquered the Sikh empire in 1849, they recruited large numbers of Sikhs into the British Indian Army. They fought for the empire around the world, including in the First and Second Opium Wars in China. In World War One, they fought on the Western Front in France and, in World War Two, they served in the Allied invasion of Italy. They accounted for 60 per cent of the Indian forces who resisted Japan's attacks on what is today Malaysia and Singapore. In December 1941, many died defending Hong Kong against Japanese forces.

Like the Parsees, they were here in the early years of the British colony. Sikh soldiers were present at the flag-raising ceremony in January 1841. In 1844, according to Hong Kong government records, a British police officer formed a night patrol of 23 Indians, including Sikhs; they were posted on Queen's Road, in Central, and were effective in reducing crime. For the British rulers, Sikh policemen had much to recommend them; they were tall and muscular, towering over the smaller Cantonese residents of Hong Kong. They had colourful turbans and black beards, making them even more imposing.

The British sent officers from home to run their police force but could not afford to send enough men to fill the lower ranks. So they used a mixture of Indians and Chinese men. The Chinese had the advantage of local knowledge and mastery of the Cantonese dialect spoken in Hong Kong, but they were vulnerable to pressure from family and clan and sometimes gambling and criminal syndicates. Sikhs, on the other hand, did not have such local links and would be more loyal to the power that had recruited them. In June 1867, a new Sikh contingent of 148 policemen arrived in Hong Kong; they had been recruited from Amritsar and the surrounding areas. In 1869, the government set up schools to teach the new recruits to speak Cantonese. From 1870, many Sikhs transferred to the prison service, to work as guards. The original contract was five years of service, followed by eight months of home leave, and a pension after 10 years. They were not allowed to marry in Hong Kong or bring their wives with them; they had to live in cramped conditions, sometimes eight to ten men in one small apartment. They worked shifts and shared beds, cooking and cleaning duties. They brought with them their love and mastery of hockey, and this has lasted up to today. By 1897, there were 226 Sikh policemen and by 1920 the total had risen to 477. According to the tally at the end of World War Two, there were 774 Indian policemen, mostly Sikhs, out of a total force of 2,220. After completing their service, the Sikhs, like other Indians, had the option of going home or staying in Hong Kong; a majority chose the latter because life in the Punjab was hard. Those who stayed on worked as guards and watchmen. Sikhs also served as soldiers. The Hong Kong Regiment, which served from 1892 to 1902, included five companies of Punjabis.

→ *Gurudwara – Spiritual and Community Centre*

The Khalsa Diwan Sikh Temple in Wan Chai is their religious centre. It was built in 1901 by Sikhs serving in the British Army. A report in the Hong Kong Telegraph of May 12, 1902 said that the colonial government provided the land for the temple and Sikhs and Hindus in the city raised HK$10,500 needed for construction. At that time, there were about 700 Sikhs and Hindus living in Hong Kong. Every Sikh soldier, policeman and watchman was asked to give one month's pay and every merchant one month's income. The band of the Hongkong Regiment took part in the opening ceremony, a sign of the close relations between the Sikhs and the British Army. The building included a basement with a kitchen and accommodation for visitors.

"It was the first Sikh temple in Hong Kong," says Jagraj Singh, honorary secretary of the temple. "It was not only a religious site but also a gathering place for the Indian community as a whole, where people could come together from different communities. The land was given by the British authorities, at an annual rent of HK$1. The cost of building the temple was born by the members of the community. Given their small numbers and limited resources, it was an impressive effort. Since there were no suitable local candidates, the community hired a priest from Punjab on a contract of one

→ Gyani Jatinder Singh, head priest of the Gurdwara Khalsa Diwan (Sikh Temple) holds a
religious ceremony at the temple.

or two years. We have continued this system until now, hiring
a priest for one year or a maximum of two. Hindus, mainly the
Sindhi community, also come here for prayers, marriages and other
celebrations. We are in harmony with each other, even though our
religion is different."

This proved a godsend for about 5,000 Punjabis, mostly Sikhs, who
emigrated from India to Canada between 1904 and 1908. Since
there was no immigration office in India, it was the immigration
office in Hong Kong that handled the procedures they needed for
final clearance, including medical examinations, documentation and
interviews. While they were waiting, the migrants found refuge at
the temple. Its staff provided food, lodging, medical attention and
even financial assistance. It was an invaluable place of comradeship

Chapter 3 —— Sikhs – Lions and Princesses from the Punjab

and safety for those embarking on a journey that changed their life for ever. Of the 1.5 million Indians in Canada today, one-third are Sikhs. When Canadian Prime Minister Justin Trudeau announced his new 30-member cabinet in November 2015, it included four Sikhs – double the number in the Indian cabinet.

The temple added a crematorium in 1917. In 1933, because of the increase in the numbers of the community, the management committee decided to demolish the temple and build a larger one. The new temple was officially opened on April 7, 1934. In his speech at the opening ceremony, Badan Singh, chairman of the Temple Committee, said that the Sikh community in Hong Kong numbered more than 2,000, including soldiers, policemen, merchants and traders. He thanked the Hong Kong government and police force

→ A worshipper reads inside the Gurudwara Khalsa Diwan (Sikh Temple).

for their support in the rebuilding effort, according to a report in the Hong Kong Telegraph of April 9, 1934. World War Two was traumatic for the Sikh community in Hong Kong, as for the rest of the colony. In December 1941, when the invading Japanese army came across the border at Lo Wu, the Sikh Punjab Regiment was on the front line. More than 100 Sikh soldiers were killed and others were captured and imprisoned for the rest of the war. The Sikh temple continued to keep its doors open, providing refuge, food and water to those who needed it, including Chinese. It had a well which the builders had dug in September 1903 that provided much needed water throughout the war. It is still in use now.

The large number of Chinese refugees and the British flag flying over the temple attracted the attention of Japanese pilots who dropped two bombs on the building, causing extensive damage and killing the head priest as well as a number of others inside. After the war, the temple was rebuilt by the Sikhs with help from their Hindu neighbours.

The colonial government continued to hire Punjabi Sikhs and Muslims for the police and prison service, with 60 recruited in early 1947 and brought to Hong Kong.

The Partition of British India was a tragedy for the Punjab. It was divided down the middle, with the western half going to Pakistan and the eastern half going to India. Thousands of Sikhs in the western half who did not want to live in the new Muslim state left with whatever they could carry, bidding farewell to their land, homes and possessions to make a new life elsewhere. They were promised land to compensate them for what they had lost, but many did not receive it. "We in Hong Kong were not affected directly by Partition," said Jagraj Singh. "But some families had a hard time. Some in Hong Kong had to go back to help their family members in distress. The journey then took two months by boat. Most of the Sikhs in what is now Pakistan left with no more than what they could carry. A small number of the refugees came to Hong Kong to join their families here. The partition was not managed well. The British simply drew a

→ Sikh women attend a religious ceremony in the Gurudwara Khalsa Diwan (Sikh Temple).

line down the middle of Punjab. It could have been managed better."
After India became an independent state on August 15, 1947, the
new government did not allow further recruitment of its citizens for
the police in Hong Kong, but it was easy for the Sikhs of the colony
to sponsor relatives and friends to move here. So the community
continued to grow. People were happy to come since they could earn
more than at home. The new arrivals were mostly men and, like their
predecessors, they lived up to 10 in a single apartment. They held
down two or three jobs a day to earn money to send back to India
to build houses and buy farmland. The most common job was in the
security business. For many, the stay in Hong Kong was short-term, a
precious opportunity to earn money.

The foundation of the People's Republic in 1949 also caused an increase in the Sikh population of China. There was a community that had been living in Shanghai for a century; they had gone there for the same reasons as their fellow Sikhs in Hong Kong. In 1940, there were 557 Sikhs living there; most working as policemen, others as security guards at warehouses and big companies. A few made their living as money-lenders. They had built a Gurudwara, measuring 1,500 square metres, on 326 Dongbaoxing Road. It served as a religious and community centre. The 1949 revolution forced all the Sikhs to leave Shanghai; most fled to Hong Kong. They arrived penniless. Many stayed at the Sikh temple and remained for a long time until they could find jobs and make a life for themselves in this new city.

For the Sikhs who had been long settled in Hong Kong, job prospects were better. Those who were educated and spoke Cantonese and English worked in government departments, such as the Post Office, Radio Hong Kong (now Radio Television Hong Kong), the courts, the auxiliary police, and the Correctional Services Department (CSD). Some followed their fathers and grandfathers into the same government offices. Ish Kumar Bhagat reached the rank of Assistant Commissioner of the CSD. The British used many Sikh soldiers to guard the arms and ammunition used by their security forces that were stored on Stonecutters Island. This was a sign of confidence in their loyalty and vigilance. They also had another valuable asset when it came to the safe handling of ammunition: they were non-smokers. They were given there a room to use as a Gurudwara, where they offered prayers each day. Two years ahead of the 1997 handover, the British moved the depot out of Hong Kong; the Sikh soldiers were demobilised and given golden handshakes.

The most senior Sikh in government service under the British was Harnam Singh Grewal. He was born in Hong Kong in December 1937 and spent most of his childhood in his ancestral village in the Punjab, where he attended primary school. In 1947, his family returned to Hong Kong, where he continued his education. He earned two degrees from the University of Hong Kong, before studying for two years at Cambridge University. After his return to Hong Kong, he joined the government as an administrative officer in 1964 and rose to senior positions, including Commissioner of Customs and Excise and Secretary for Transport. In February 1987, he became secretary for the Civil Service, putting him in charge of the city's civil servants – one of the top positions in the government. This was the highest position achieved by a Sikh during the 155 years of British rule. In April 1990, Grewal retired on medical grounds and went to live in Canada. He was also an active member of the Royal Hong Kong Regiment (Volunteers) for 21 years and played for the Hong Kong hockey team at the 1964 Tokyo Olympics. In 1990, the British government awarded him a CBE (Commander of the British Empire) medal.

The most famous Sikh company in Hong Kong is the Thakral Group. It was set up in 1905, to trade textile products made in Thailand, and listed its shares on the Singapore stock market in 1995. With a market capitalisation of over US$400 million, it was the biggest listing of that year. In 2017, it reported annual turnover of 153.2 million Singapore dollars. Today it is a multinational corporation with operations in 40 countries. It has two divisions – lifestyle and investment. Its lifestyle division markets and distributes brands in the beauty, wellness and lifestyle sectors, through e-commerce as well as traditional retailers. Its investment division invests directly or with partners in real estate and other areas, in Hong Kong, mainland China, Japan, Australia and elsewhere. In 2005, it moved its operational headquarters to Hong Kong.

→ *Handover*

As for the other minority communities, the handover to China in 1997 was a turning point. "This was a very big event. No-one knew what would happen," says Jagraj Singh. "About 500 families – 2,000-3,000 people – left to join their relatives in Canada, Europe or elsewhere. But they kept their properties here. Most came back when they saw that things had not changed. Only a very few left for good." After the handover, the Special Administrative Region Government

→ A Sikh reads from the Sikh holy scripture.

introduced a regulation requiring applicants to read and write Chinese as a condition of entry. The majority of Sikhs, like other people of South Asian origin, were unable to meet this requirement, so new recruitment stopped. Chinese had replaced English as the most important language of government. Those already working within the government kept their posts and were not affected; but their promotion was limited if they did not know written Chinese. Top posts were reserved for those holding a Chinese passport. Historically, Sikhs have had a close connection with the Correctional Services Department. Each November, Sikhs who had retired from the department and moved abroad, mostly in Canada, returned to Hong Kong to celebrate a religious festival at the Gurudwara. In November 2010, Sin Yat-kin, commissioner of the CSD, visited the temple to see his former, as well as current, employees. Before

Chapter 3 —— Sikhs – Lions and Princesses from the Punjab

his visit, he announced that the CSD would resume recruitment of Sikhs, with a requirement of a low standard of written Chinese but fluency in speaking.

But, while the door for many government jobs closed, the Sikhs moved smoothly into the private sector. Those who had lived for generations in the city benefited from its good education system to join professions that their grandparents had only dreamt of – finance, medicine, accountancy, teaching, the media, insurance, law, and engineering. Jaspal Singh Bindra became chief executive for Asia of the Standard Chartered Bank in Hong Kong, from which he stepped down in February 2016; he worked in the bank for more than 16 years.

In social terms, the Sikhs remain conservative. Members of the community prefer their young people to marry other Sikhs, either residents of Hong Kong or spouses arranged from India. The SAR Government accepts this arrangement and grants immigration visas to such spouses.

→ *Building a New Gurudwara*

The community has just embarked on an ambitious project – the largest redevelopment of the temple in its history. "Recently, we discovered that the structure was weak as cracks appeared in its walls," said Jagraj Singh. "The Sikh community unanimously decided to demolish the existing temple and build a larger one. This involved many hurdles because the government had listed this as a heritage building. Finally, we received government approval. The redevelopment project will cost HK$170 million, donations received mainly from Sikhs and Hindus communities. So far we have raised HK$100 million and have not asked for help from people in the Punjab. People are attached to this place, the centre of our community. I, for example, am the fourth generation of my family. The new building will have four storeys, including two prayer halls, a social hall, kitchen, dining hall, tutorial classrooms, a kindergarten and a car park. In a Sikh Temple, men and women pray together."

→ Sikh workers gather inside the part of the temple which is being rebuilt.

The temple offers free meals and short-term accommodation to international visitors of any faith. "Our langar – free kitchen— is open to everyone for a free meal seven days a week," said Jagraj Singh. "When the UK consulate has a British citizen who needs such accommodation, they call us and we provide it." The main holy days and festivals are the birthday of Guru Nanak, founder of the faith, and Guru Gobind Singh, the 10th guru: and Baisakhi – the birthday of all Sikhs. The temple provides lessons in music, religious and academic subjects, martial arts and the Punjabi language. It also runs a kindergarten and a library.

The community plans a second temple in Hong Kong, in the Tung Chung district, close to the city's airport; it is a 40-km journey to the existing Gurudwara. In 2004, Sikhs living there began to negotiate with the SAR Government for a plot of land to build a temple.

"The first Guru Nanak Dev Ji, born in 1469, saw inequality around him," says Mr Singh. He believed in human equality and inner human values. So he founded a religion with no caste. After baptism, a male Sikh is given the middle name of 'Singh' (lion) and a female Sikh the middle name of 'Kaur' (crown prince). In a Gurudwara, you must put aside caste thinking; in the prayer hall, we are all the same. The guru forbids alcohol and tobacco.

"The main prayers (in the Gurudwara) are on Sunday mornings, when 1,000 people come. We are authorised by the Hong Kong government to perform weddings. We recently had a marriage ceremony for one prominent family – over 1,000 people attended.

→ A priest gives Karah Parshad, a sweet vegetarian pudding, to a Sikh man after a religious ceremony at the temple.

On Sundays, we also have classes in the Punjabi language, the recitation of prayers and martial arts classes. During the summer, we hold these classes daily, because the children do not attend school. Health check-up camps, job fairs and other information seminars are regularly held at the Gurdwara by various local organisations.

"Most of those who came in the 19th century stayed here. At that time, living conditions in Punjab were not so favourable. The British government here allowed them to stay. They were first recruited as soldiers and then as policemen. They were good because of their bravery, loyalty and sincerity, the virtues taught to us by the Guru. They adopted Hong Kong as their home. The soldiers brought their siblings with them. They worked here as watchmen and security guards and majority lived in Wan Chai, close to the temple. I have not heard of the Indian mutiny (a rebellion in India in 1857 against British rule) having any impact in Hong Kong. One of their jobs was to guard the ammunition depots of the British Army at Stonecutters' Island. Since Sikhs do not smoke, they made the fire risk minimal. The second generation became office clerks, managers and then ran their own businesses. Now they are running trading firms, set up during the last 50-60 years. According to custom and family tradition, we marry only Sikhs. If you marry a non-Sikh, he or she must convert to Sikhism. The process is not complicated."

What was the impact of 1997? "This was a very big event. No-one knew what would happen. About 500 families – 2,000-3,000 people – left to join their relatives in Canada, Europe or elsewhere. But they kept their properties here. Most came back when they saw that things had not changed. Only a very few left for good.

"After 1997, the rules changed. Those who applied for government jobs have to pass an exam in written Chinese that did not exist before 1997. This was equivalent to Hong Kong Secondary School Education Examination (Form 5). During our schooling we were not taught Chinese, we could speak but not read or write Chinese. At that time Chinese was not mandatory. Those who were already in the government were able to keep their jobs. This change was expected

→ A woman feeds a boy with free food provided by the Sikh Temple.

and was not a surprise. Hong Kong had become part of China again. One Indian staff of the Correctional Services Department, Gurcharan Singh Galib, needed to pass the exam to get promoted. So he took courses and he passed the exam; he got his promotion.

"Not much has changed since 1997. Our community, like others, has the same life as before."

What passports do you hold? "The British Government was very generous and gave Indians full UK passports to holders of British National (Overseas) passport holders. In 1995, we received full UK passports. Many have bought a house in the UK but not emigrated. My son has a full UK passport but not my daughter, who has an Indian one. When she was born, I did not have a full UK passport."

Why is there communal harmony in Hong Kong? "After the Indian Army stormed the Golden Temple in Amritsar (in an attack on the holy site to remove a militant religious leader and his armed followers in June 1984), we wrote petitions to the Indian consulate and protested. This hurt our religious sentiments; our brothers and sisters had been killed. If there are cases of violence in Hong Kong, they are isolated and the work of individual people. The aim of each religion is to be good; they are meant to be peaceful.

Is it hard to keep young Sikhs in the faith? "Young people are faced with globalisation and move away from the Sikh teaching. Because they come to the temple when they were young, they understand everything. This phase is temporary. We are doing a good job to uphold our values and beliefs."

---

1. Interview with Jagraj Singh, honorary secretary of Sikh Gurudwara (25/4/2018)

2. "Sikhs in Hong Kong" by Gulbir Singh Batra and published by Sri Guru Gobind Singh Educational Trust, Hong Kong, and Khalsa Diwan (Sikh Temple) of Hong Kong

Policeman Who Guarded Ammunition on Stonecutters Island

Gill Sukha Singh

→ Gill Sukha Singh at the family house in Park Island, Ma Wan.

Gill Sukha Singh is a retired British Army policeman and former president of the Sikh temple. Born in Hong Kong in August 1939, he left for India with his family after Japanese forces occupied the territory in World War Two, returning as a young man in 1960.

"I was born in Hung Hom at Green Island Cement Company. That was where my father worked after he left the British Army, which I would later also join. I joined as a private and when I retired from the army I was a staff sergeant, with three stripes [on the shoulder of his uniform] and one crown."

Mr Singh sits with his oldest son, a doctor, at their home in Park Island, Ma Wan. On a big screen television they watch Sikh priests at the Golden Temple in Amritsar in India's northwest, as they sing and conduct prayers. Mr Singh would work for Hong Kong's Army Depot Police (ADP) for 34 years at the ammunition bunkers on Stonecutters Island until the unit was disbanded in 1993 ahead of the 1997 handover.

"It was a separate island then," says Mr Singh. "Now it is part of the mainland. Anyone who came within 100 yards,

we would arrest them." He lived on Stonecutters Island for five years, but then moved to the more convenient Wan Chai after getting married.

Mr Singh's mother was Chinese and he speaks fluent Cantonese. It was not uncommon, he says, for Sikh men to marry local Chinese women as they were usually here by themselves. His mother, Rattan Kaur, moved to India with her family in 1946 and remained there after her husband died in 1952. "She loved India. She was Chinese but she was pure Punjabi!" says Mr Singh.

"When I returned here in 1960, Hong Kong was very different. The buildings only really went up to seven storeys and the harbour was still very big" ahead of the more recent stages of land reclamation. During the war, he says, he lived with his mother in the Khalsa Diwan (Hong Kong) Sikh Temple in Wan Chai. "I owe those days to my mother, for giving me the food that sustained me. We stayed at the Gurudwara [temple] during the war and the building was bombed. Part of the Gurudwara was damaged but there were no casualties."

Mr Singh's job in the ADP involved guarding

→ Gill Sukha Singh and his new wife Pritam Kaur Gill, shortly after their wedding in India in 1965. This was taken at a studio in Hong Kong.

→ Gill Sukha Singh on Stonecutters Island.

the ammunition. An old photograph on the coffee table shows him in khaki shorts and shirt on the island. When he headed back to India on six months' home leave in 1965 his mother introduced him to his future wife, Pritam Kaur Gill.

In the album on the coffee table are photos of their wedding in her home village of Dhaul Kalan near Amritsar in Punjab. Mr Singh wore a suit and his bride was dressed in a red sari. He describes how they went to the temple and had to walk round the Sikh holy book – the Guru Granth Sahib – four times. The priest then read from the sacred text.

On Stonecutters Island, Mr Singh would play volleyball with his colleagues. "During the riots in 1967 we were on standby at Stonecutters Island and weren't allowed to go anywhere. We had to be at the ready 24 hours a day, just in case we were needed. In the end, it wasn't required."

"Dad has a lot of fond memories of working at the Army Depot Police," says his oldest son Dr. Narindar Pal Singh Gill. "They would have a big New Year party, where they would invite all the British officers. They would first have the three-day traditional New Year celebrations at the Gurudwara, which the ADP staff would pay for. And this tradition continued after they were disbanded. Even in April this year the Visaki was still organized by the former staff members of the ADP. And then, in the old days, they would have a big party in the mess at Stonecutters Island."

"We would invite all the army staff from the headquarters and other places of the British Army," says his father. "Everything would be free for them on this party with us. Food. Drink. Curry chicken, samosas, pakoras. They joined in on everything!"

After the ADP was disbanded in 1993, Mr Singh joined a French construction company, Dragages, to oversee their security guards. "After that I joined a new import-export company that was making CDs at Sha Tin," before retiring in 2001.

He has three children and enjoys his role as father and grandfather, looking at the next generations who have been able to benefit from tertiary education and go on to professional careers.

"My son, Narindar, is the first Sikh doctor in Hong Kong," he says proudly.

Gurkhas – Protecting the Border, Keeping the Peace

Gurkhas- Protecting the Border, Keeping the Peace

One important element of the South Asian community in Hong Kong are the Nepalis, who number 20,000-30,000. They are Gurkhas, one of the most famous regiments of the British Army and their descendants. They served in the city in the colonial period and now work as security men, bodyguards, drivers and on construction sites. In many cases their limited knowledge of written and spoken Chinese and a lack of higher education often makes it difficult for them to obtain white-collar jobs and raise their income and social status.

The Gurkhas began their long association with the British Army in 1815, after European officers became aware of their exceptional fighting qualities. They served the British crown in countries all over the world. During World War One, more than 200,000 Gurkhas fought for Britain; they suffered about 20,000 casualties and won

→ Ex-Gurkhas Jasin Chamling, Khamba Sing Gurung, and Juna Raj Ale march after paying respects to their departed comrades at the Gurkha Cemetery in Hong Kong.

nearly 2,000 gallantry awards. During World War Two, the number increased to more than 250,000, with 32,000 casualties. They fought in North Africa, Syria, Italy and Greece and against the Japanese in Burma, northeast India and Singapore. In total, over 50,000 died fighting for the British Crown; 13 were awarded the Victoria Cross, the highest award given for valour by the British Government.

They first arrived in Hong Kong from Malaya in 1948 on rotation during a communist insurgency known as the Malayan Emergency. It became their home base in 1969-70 when their training depot was relocated here from Sungai Petani, in Kedah state in Malaya.

→ (Top) Gurkha Cemetery at Tam Mei in the New Territories.

→ (Bottom) Relatives pay respect to their relatives at the Gurkha Cemetery at Tam Mei in the New Territories.

"The Emergency had run down," said Nigel Collett, a former British Army officer. "It was time to station them somewhere else." He came to know the Gurkhas well during a long and distinguished military career. After attending the Royal Military Academy in Sandhurst, he served in Britain, Oman and Zimbabwe, then attended the Army Staff College. In 1984, he was promoted to major and transferred to the 6th Queen Elizabeth's Own Gurkha Rifles and posted to Hong Kong. He served there from 1985 to 1992; he was promoted to lieutenant-colonel and put in command of the 6th in 1991. In 1994, he published a Nepali-English dictionary which has been used by the British Army. He has lived in Hong Kong since 1995.

After the Gurkhas were posted here, their main responsibility was patrolling the border with the mainland to prevent the entry of illegal immigrants. This was particularly important during the chaotic years of the Cultural Revolution (1966-76) when social order broke down in many parts of China. "The Gurkhas were good peacetime soldiers. They were very disciplined, obeyed orders and (were) polite to people," says Collett. "They treated Chinese illegals with respect and without violence, unlike some of the British soldiers. They were very happy to be posted here." The Gurkhas were also used to control angry crowds during the Star Ferry riots of 1966. As troops serving the government, they lived like other British soldiers, apart from the local community. They lived in camps with their own kindergartens, schools, restaurants, temples and sports grounds as well as other facilities. Opportunities to learn Cantonese and mix with the local Chinese population were limited. Those with the rank of sergeant or above were allowed to bring their families with them; those of lower rank had to leave them at home in Nepal except for one tour of three years. "The camps were like Gurkha villages," said Collett. "They had everything they needed. They were very peaceful. We celebrated the Hindu festivals. They had large families; the mothers enjoyed excellent pre- and post-natal care at the British Military Hospital." Those born in Hong Kong earned the right of permanent residency. Marriages were usually arranged by their families, according to the ethnic group and caste to which they belonged. "We lived an insular life inside the barracks," says Collett. "The Gurkhas did not want

→ Members of the Gurkha Transport Regiment practise internal security duties on the streets of Hong Kong in a Saracen armoured car. The photograph was taken in the late 1980s.

to mix with the Chinese. We hardly even mixed with other British soldiers."

But things changed in the 1990s. Hong Kong was to return to China in 1997 and there was no place for Gurkhas in the Chinese army to be stationed here. After the collapse of the Berlin Wall in 1989 and the break-up of the Soviet Union in 1991, Britain, like other Western countries, decided that it did not need such a large army; this was the "peace dividend". British regiments lobbied fiercely to be saved, even in a reduced form, and argued that foreign soldiers like the Gurkhas should be laid off before British ones. They won the argument. So as a lieutenant-colonel and commanding officer, Collett had the unenviable task of deciding who should be dismissed; he had to break the bad news to men with whom he had served for many years.

"We considered criteria like medical condition, ability and age. In Brunei, after 1992, I had 20 people queuing up outside my door each fortnight and I had to tell them they would be laid off. Everyone felt sad." The outlook for those let go was not good. A career in the Nepali army was not available and offered a low salary and worse conditions of service than those they were used to. The Indian army was not recruiting Gurkhas of the age of those discharged. Jobs in Nepal were, as they are now, hard to find and badly paid. The only bright spot was recruiting by the Sultan of Brunei for his Gurkha Reserve Unit: and Jardine's, one of the city's oldest British companies, hiring several thousand Gurkhas as security guards for its many properties here. Those born in Hong Kong had the option to stay and make a new life outside the army camp. Many moved to Kam Tin, a village near their base, and Yuen Long. They took jobs as

→ Gurkha soldiers practise shooting after a long-distance run.

Chapter 4 —— Gurkhas – Protecting the Border, Keeping the Peace

3

4

security guards, valets, bodyguards, drivers and on construction sites. A plum job was to serve as one of the bodyguards of Li Ka-shing, Hong Kong's richest man; he has been guarded by former Gurkhas for more than 20 years. Under the terms of the handover, Nepalese could not apply for a Chinese passport even if they had the right of permanent residence. They hold Nepalese passports.

Those not born in Hong Kong did not have the right to stay, even if they had lived here for more than the seven years it normally takes a foreigner to obtain an identity card for permanent residence. This was because, like other British soldiers, the Gurkhas did not have to go through Hong Kong immigration on entering or leaving the colony; so there was no record of how long they had lived here. At that time Britain, the country they had served for nearly 200 years, did not offer them the choice to settle there. So the only option for those unable to stay here and unable to find work elsewhere was to return to Nepal, one of the world's poorest countries with low salaries and limited employment prospects. In November 1996, seven months before the handover, the Gurkha base here closed and moved to Britain; most of the remaining soldiers left.

Many officers in the Gurkha regiments have a strong sense of loyalty and affection toward the men and women who served under them.

→ Former governor Sir David Wilson attends a ceremony in Hong Kong to award a Victoria Cross to a Gurkha soldier. Nigel Collett was behind Wilson, to the left.

Some decided that they must help the Gurkhas and their descendants find a place in the new post-1997 world. Nigel Collett was one of them. He left the British Army in 1994 after serving in Brunei. "We decided to try to help them find work. Our idea was to send them to sea – that was a new concept," he said. "The benefits of this were that they did not need a visa, paid no tax on their income and had work for a period of eight months." So he set up a company in Kathmandu, the capital of Nepal, and began to market retired Gurkhas to international cruise companies, as security guards, stewards and workers in restaurants, kitchens, bars and cleaning operations. After 10 months, he moved to Hong Kong where he set up the Gurkha International Group to continue his work and provide reputable employment for the Nepalis in the city and around the world. In Hong Kong, the company recruits and provides security guards, drivers, bodyguards and personal staff; those hired have Hong Kong identity cards and the right to work in the city. The group is a member of the Hong Kong General Chamber of Commerce, the Employers' Federation of Hong Kong and the Hong Kong Security Association. It also finds work for Nepalis outside Hong Kong, such as in the casinos of Macau and on international cruise liners. His firm is paid a commission for those job placements. After a humble beginning, his company has prospered. It has found jobs for more than 10,000 Nepalis and currently manages 920 on cruise ships in addition to employing 100 in its Hong Kong office. "I live in a Nepali bubble. We have an office in Kathmandu. My life is Nepali," he said.

In 1999, the Hong Kong government closed the door to new immigration from Nepal. Since then, it has only allowed entry to those born here with a right of permanent residence or those coming to marry a permanent resident. This followed a serious scandal of fake documents, including Hong Kong birth certificates and those showing service as a Gurkha. They were produced by forgers in Nepal and Hong Kong – many operating out of the Chunking Mansions. Many companies made hiring decisions based on these fraudulent documents. "The number of these forgeries may have reached as many as 20,000," said Collett. "In Nepal… you can buy documents and pay officials. It is very unregulated. Families change identities." This scandal seriously affected the Hong Kong government's attitude toward Nepalis.

After 1997, it became an issue as to whether the Gurkhas would be allowed to settle in Britain. It was controversial. On the one side was a government that wanted to limit the number of new immigrants; on the other was the moral obligation toward those who had fought, and died, for Britain for nearly two centuries. Until 2004, Gurkhas were not allowed to settle in the U.K. That year, the government changed the rules; those who had retired after 1997 would be given that right. After a court challenge and a well-organised public campaign led by actress Joana Lumley, the daughter of a Gurkha officer, the government gave a further concession. In May 2009, the British Home Secretary announced that all Gurkha veterans who retired before 1997 with at least four years' service would be allowed to settle in the UK. After this decision, several thousand Gurkhas in Hong Kong left for Britain. They preferred a country with which they felt familiar; they spoke the language and there was a long-established Nepali community. Their children had a better future. In Hong Kong, many feel they are outsiders, belonging to neither the Chinese nor the expatriate communities.

The Nepalis here are at a disadvantage compared to the Indians and Pakistanis whose ancestors have been in the city for generations. These ties over the years have enabled them to build businesses and wealth, put down roots and connections and attain fluency in Cantonese. But the Nepalis arrived only at the end of the 1960s and lived in army barracks, separated from the local community. They earned only the modest incomes of low-ranking soldiers. With the return of Hong Kong to China, they lost their military identity and had to make a new life in one of the world's most expensive and competitive cities. Their biggest handicap is a lack of fluency in Cantonese, the Chinese dialect spoken in Hong Kong. Their native language is that of their ethnic group; then they learn Nepali, the national language of their native country. Those who are permanent residents in Hong Kong have the right to attend government schools where instruction is mainly in Cantonese, with some teaching in English. Education in international English-language schools is extremely expensive and out of reach of nearly all Nepali families. The system is highly competitive, with exams at every stage. Entrance into Hong Kong tertiary education requires a high-level of written and spoken Chinese or English.

"Many Nepali children attend Cantonese schools but fall behind. Many go back to Nepal to study. But its diplomas are not recognised here. So, if they graduate from university there, their qualifications are no use in Hong Kong. They are likely to end up on construction sites," says Collett. He said that the government had not addressed the issue seriously for 20 years. "If it had invested the money and resources in teaching Chinese to the Nepalis, they would do well and get white-collar jobs. They like the climate here and it is only five hours' flight from

→ (Top) Lieutenant-Colonel Nigel Collett.

→ (Bottom) Nigel Collett briefs ex-Gukhas who work as security guards at Fanling Golf Club.

→ (Top) A Hindu devotee, Kanya Chauhan, pays
homage at a shrine at the Hindu Temple.

→ (Bottom) Ms Chauhan has mehndi on her
hands, an ancient Indian form of henna art.

Nepal. They would like to stay."

→ *Religion in Nepal*

Nepal is a country of many religions that have been practised for centuries. According to the 2011 census, Hindus accounted for more than 80 per cent of the population. Buddhism is practised by about nine per cent, Islam 4.4 per cent, Christianity 1.4 per cent and Kiratism – the religion of the Kirati tribes – three per cent. Before the overthrow of King Gyanendra in 2008, Nepal was officially a Hindu kingdom. A new constitution adopted in 2015 guarantees freedom of religion. Religion is not only a set of beliefs and rituals but a mixture of traditions, festivals and doctrines. They play a central role in society and the lives of people.

Prince Siddhartha, the birth name of the Lord Buddha, was born in 623 B.C. in what is now Lumbini in the Rupandehi district of Nepal. His birthplace has become a place of pilgrimage for believers from around the world. He conducted most of his mission in India. In Nepal, Hinduism and Buddhism have adopted many of the tenets of the other religion; often they share the same deities and temples and followers of the two worship together. Over the centuries, the two have never engaged in religious conflict. The county is home

to many fine examples of Hindu and Buddhist art and sculpture. It has three main schools of Buddhism – Tibetan, Newar (a form of Vajrayana) and Theravada.

As in India, another country with a Hindu majority, Nepal has a caste system, with four major castes. It persists despite efforts to reduce its importance. Education is free and open to all castes. In 1962, the government passed a law making it illegal to discriminate against other castes. But the higher castes continue to dominate administration, the economy and higher education; they have on average higher incomes than lower castes.

When Nepalese live abroad, they take their religion and festivals with them. So it is with the community in Hong Kong.

1.   Interview with Nigel Collett

More than 30 Years of Service in Hong Kong

Major Balkrishna Rana

→ Major Balkrishna Rana, MBE, in his Gurkha uniform.

When Balkrishna Rana joined the British Army in 1956, World War Two was still very much in people's memories. Where he was a teenager growing up in rural western Nepal, a life in the army promised a ticket for travel and new opportunities; it was far more attractive to many of the young men in the village than a gruelling life in the fields.

Now a retired major in Kathmandu, he recalls his first stint in the army in north Malaya, in what is Malaysia today. He travelled for three days by train through India, 14 days by sea and then a short train ride again from Butterworth to Sungai Petani in Malaya. He underwent training for three years before he joined the regiment in Hong Kong in 1960. While the name of his regiment has changed frequently, he says, at the time it was the Gurkha Army Service Corps. At that point, it was the youngest regiment in the Brigade of Gurkhas.

"My sub-unit was the 28 Company Gurkha Army Service Corps," he says. "I grew up mostly in the hills. I was in India when my father was in the British Indian Army. He retired shortly after the war and I went back to our home village at five or six years old."

The village was called Tanahunsur in the district of Tanahun, a world away from Hong Kong. But there were plenty of hills in Hong Kong for him to run across. In fact, Major Rana reckons he's reached the top of most of Hong Kong's hills either for army training or just for fun.

"I used to run a lot, for exercise, for competitions, orienteering and exercise. A lot of [army] exercises involved getting up on the hills and then charging back down them. I was very competitive, had to be on top."

In the Army Service Corps, there were two service components – one was supplies, the other transport. As a young soldier, Major Rana would often drive a truck or another vehicle of the regiment. It became second nature, and now he misses it at times. In his army days, he was based in Hong Kong with occasional trips away. Some of his fellow soldiers were sent off to Australia or New Zealand on exercises or on courses to the UK.

The Brigade of Gurkhas made Hong Kong its home in 1971 with its training depot at Shek Kong in the New Territories. The battalions took turns in posting to the UK and Brunei. From the UK, they went to Belize, Cyprus and, famously, to the Falklands War. In November 1981, Major Rana was transferred to the 2/7th Duke of Edinburgh's Own Gurkha Rifles, based at Lyemun Barracks (Lei Yue Mun). They were visited by Prince Philip during a royal tour in 1986. "My regiment made history for itself by having been chosen to deploy and excelling during the first Gulf War in 1991, when it deployed as 28 (Ambulance) Squadron GTR from Hong Kong," he said. Peacetime work for the Gurkha units involved helping rescue efforts during typhoons and landslides. Major Rana recalls Typhoon Wanda in 1962, when an entire village of boatpeople was swept away in Tai Po, and the deadly Po Shan Road landslide in Mid-Levels in 1972. The troops were also involved in internal security and border protection, plus raising funds for the Community Chest of Hong Kong.

When Major Rana arrived in Hong Kong in 1960, he lived in what is now Kowloon Park. His unit shared the camp with the Brigade and Garrison Headquarters. "We were in Whitfield Barracks for 10 years." He then moved to Sham Shui Po and on to Shek Kong, when the whole Brigade of Gurkhas converged. Born in 1941, Major Rana married in Nepal in 1964. "After the marriage we were separated for nearly four

years, and then she was able to join me. After that, because of my seniority, she was with me all the time until we left in 1992." He said that Shek Kong was a close-knit Nepalese community that enjoyed good relations with British families but did not have much to do with local Chinese residents.

The Gurkhas are famous for their kukri knives. They are not dissimilar to a machete and are used as both a tool and weapon in Nepal. "In the army, one was issued with one. One had to use it and train with it and at war time it became second nature, especially in close combat situations. So one didn't think about what to do, a way to get out of a mess in a tight situation," he says. The kukri is both a symbol and useful weapon for Gurkhas. "The Gurkhas with their kukris in hand charging the enemy as last resort became very famous during the two World Wars."

"Important Hindu festivals such as the Dashain festival that falls in October, and Tihar, the five-day festival of lights in Nepal, would be formal regimental affairs. The whole idea of making it so formal and regimental was because the Gurkhas had for many years been stationed in foreign countries during the First and Second

World Wars in battlefield areas.

So, by ensuring that they could celebrate their festivals together, the military could give them a sense of being at home and mitigate the homesickness of not marking these festivals in their native Nepalese mountains."

Looking back at his more than three decades of military service in Hong Kong, Major Rana says he misses the city. "I was there for so many years with the children. Just looking out, I could tell what land feature was named what. Then there was the shopping, and the water sports. We have mountains but no sea in Nepal."

Major Rana says the high point of his army life was a visit to the UK in July 1991 with his family, where he was awarded The Most Excellent Order of the British Empire (MBE) at Buckingham Palace by Queen Elizabeth II. These days, he is the general secretary of the Regimental Association Nepal and president of his own regiment. He proudly says that his regiment has been now re-designated as the Queen's Own Gurkha Logistic Regiment. Both these appointments in Nepal give him plenty to do to help keep his mind away from nostalgia for his youth.

"I was sad to leave Hong Kong in 1992. I had been there for a very long time, so leaving it was something of a cultural shock. But life goes on. Moving to a similar set up in Brunei being with the Gurkhas helped to mitigate those feelings." But Major Rana, a grandfather, still enjoys returning to Hong Kong to see his three children and their families at least once a year.

→ Major Balkrishna Rana, MBE and his wife Bhim Kumari Rana, at Buckingham Palace in 1991.

Protecting Hong Kong from Illegal Immigrants

Captain Nam Sing Thapa Magar

→ Captain Nam Sing Thapa Magar, was stationed at the Gallipoli Barracks, San Wai Camp, in Hong Kong in 1962.

"There was more than a brigade of Chinese soldiers on the other side of the border in mainland China. Some trained their rifles at me, ready to fire at any moment. If they had pulled the trigger, I would not be talking to you today. We had guns but no ammunition. I was afraid."

Nam Sing Thapa, 72, was describing some of the events in his 24 years as a Gurkha soldier patrolling Hong Kong's border with the mainland. His career with the Gurkhas stretched from 1962 until his retirement in 1986. Now he lives with his family in a cramped apartment on a tumbledown street in Lai Chi Kok. "Our 48 Brigade record was catching more than 16,000 illegals in one month. We gave them over to the Hong Kong police, to be handed over to the Chinese authorities. The Gurkhas patrolled the border 24 hours a day, seven days a week, manning the observation and listening posts – watching and listening. We were not allowed to shoot. I never shot or wounded anyone."

He was one of thousands of Gurkha soldiers who patrolled the border, assisting the Hong Kong police. "Today I receive a pension from the Gurkhas, one-third of that given to British members of the regiment. It is not enough to live on. I have

to do other work. I plan to return to Nepal in one or two years. I have a small plot of land there. But we have a Communist government now there. What is it going to do?"

Nam was born in February 1946 in the Syanja district in central Nepal. His father was a warrant officer in the Gurkhas who served from 1942 to 1966. At the age of four, he was helping his grandfather look after cows, goats and buffaloes on the mountain sides. "I used to cry because of the difficulties of controlling the animals who damaged crops," he says. In 1953, he went with his father to the Gurkha camp in what was then Malaya (now Malaysia). "There was no transportation and no roads. So we had to walk from the village to the Paklihawa British recruiting camp; it took six days. Then we got in a truck to Gorakhpur in India. From there we took a train to Calcutta, where we boarded a ship to Malaya. His father was sent to a Gurkha camp in Ipoh. "Facilities in the camp were poor. Six to eight families shared a toilet and washrooms. We had bunk beds. At that time, dry and fresh rations were controlled – we had three ounces of meat a week, fruit once a week and rice was scarce. We had no refrigerator, so we used supplies of thick cubes of ice once a week." The young Nam

→ Captain Nam Sing Thapa Magar explains how to use a kukri knife at the Lotus Temple in Hong Kong. The Lotus Temple was built by the British for the Gurkhas and is dedicated to the God, Shiva.

attended classes at a school in the camp. In 1959, aged 13, he enlisted in the Boys' Company, the Brigade of Gurkhas, in Sungei Patani, Kedah, Malaya.

"My father insisted, saying the family needed the money. I started training in 1960. It was very tough – up at 4am, running and exercising in temperatures up to 40 degrees Celsius. We did a lot of sports, including football, volleyball, basketball, swimming, adventure training and boxing. We also did specialised training, such as First Aid, carpentry and vehicle mechanics."

In 1962, he officially joined his regiment, the second battalion 6th Queen Elizabeth's Own Gurkha Rifles; it was stationed in Gallipoli barracks, San Wai Camp beside Fanling in the New Territories. "The city was a shock – there were no trees, so we planted them. Several times bushfires broke out. We Gurkhas had to wake up at midnight and work until 4 am, walking in extended lines to put out the fire by using bamboo sticks, water buckets and so on. There was no drinking water and no baths available in 1963, so we carried stream water from the San Wai range. We Gurkhas supplied drinking water in the tanker vehicles to the village people. Hong

Kong had many tall buildings and many fishing boats. Especially during heavy rain, flooding, landslides and typhoons, we Gurkhas had to rescue the village people and fishing boat people from disasters. In emergencies, we went to rescue people and took them to safe areas; then we erected tents for immediate shelter and supplied food and drinking water. The Gurkhas built roads, bridges and houses for the village people, as needed.

"Our prime duty was to secure the border area and assist the Hong Kong police in riot control, curfews, cordons and search. It was a tough and exhausting assignment. At that time, there was no border fence, so the Gurkhas had to rely on observation posts, binoculars, eyes and quick feet. We worked in groups of four, (patrolling) five metres apart. We had kukris and a rifle, but no ammunition. Only our commander in charge had 10 rounds in his magazine which he carried. We had to use the minimum force possible. We had to concentrate our heart and mind. The illegals were inventive – they made boats out of air pillows or came over in mud boats. You could not see them until they jumped onto the land.

"We each had one bottle of water. Temperatures went up to 40 degrees Celsius. The illegals never had a weapon. If you caught one, he or she would surrender. Many tried a second or third time. In the winter, many were very cold. I remember a woman of 18-19 years; she was shivering. I gave her tea and my sleeping bag for the night, before we handed her over the police." The brigade record was 16,000 captured in a single month.

Boxing at the Tokyo Olympics

Nam was a talented sportsman and excelled at boxing. A flyweight, he started boxing in 1960 at the camp in Malaya and continued at the barracks in Hong Kong two years later. He boxed for Battalion, Land Forces then the Far East Land Forces Individual Championships in Singapore; he won the Far East Land Forces (All India Silver belt), as well as exhibition matches. His commanders recommended him to the Nepali government for inclusion in their team for the Tokyo Olympics in 1964. He received a letter of encouragement from the then ruler of Nepal, King Mahendra. "We were the first Nepalis to represent our country at the Olympics. There were four of us boxers and two marathon runners. I was unlucky. My first fight was against a black American who had won the bronze

→ (Top) Captain Nam Sing Thapa Magar shows his kukri knife in front of the Lotus Temple in Hong Kong.

→ (Bottom) Captain Nam Sing Thapa Magar stands inside the Lotus Temple.

medal at the 1960 Rome Olympics. I hit him with all I had but he had the ring craft. He was 33 and I was 18. The referee stopped the fight in the first round, in his favour. I was too young."

Helping Gurkha Veterans

In 1986, after 24 years of rigorous service, Nam retired from the Gurkhas at the age of 40. His officers recommended him for the post of Area Welfare Officer. These are former soldiers who live in different parts of Nepal and assist former Gurkhas who are destitute, sick or have suffered from natural disasters like fires or landslides. He accepted the post and went to live in Butwal in central Nepal, close to the border with India. "I was in charge of six districts, a very remote area, with no transportation. It took me 11 days of trekking to cover all districts. People spoke different languages, some incomprehensible." After three-and-a-half years, he resigned his post. He remained in Butwal and ran a small farm, with poultry, using knowledge he had acquired on courses in Hong Kong.

Return to Hong Kong

In 1992, he met his former regimental officer who offered him a job in Hong Kong in the security industry. The salary and conditions were too good to resist. He signed a two-year contract and returned in February 1993. He went to work for Jardine Securicor Gurkha Services Limited. Their mission was to protect the residences and properties of their clients, guard deliveries of cash and provide other security services. "Since we were in the civil service, we could not carry arms, even a kukri. All we had was a baton. We faced triads and criminal gangs." In 1996, Nam acquired a permanent residence Hong Kong identity card. He retired in 2010, at 65.

"As a former Gurkha, I am eligible for a full UK passport. My friends there have asked me to go but I said 'No, thank you'. I prefer to return to Nepal. The climate and food in the UK is not good. The weather in Nepal is nice. The money is better in Hong Kong. I have to support one sister who is unmarried and living in a village in Nepal. Our son lives in the U.S., but, with Mr. Trump, he may have to come back. Two daughters have married, one in Nepal, and one lives with us in Hong Kong. Over the next year or two, we plan to return to Nepal. We have a small plot of land there. As they say, join the British Army and go around the world – what I have done."

Community Worker

Prativa Gurung

→ Prativa Gurung enjoys a paragliding trip with an instructor on a holiday in Pokhara, Nepal.

Community worker Prativa Gurung assists local social workers in running programmes supporting young people from ethnic minorities living in the New Territories. These include young people from the Nepalese, Pakistani and Filipino communities among others.

Ms Gurung has been a community worker for two years and came here to live permanently when she was 12 years old. Now in her twenties, she helps with programmes involving volunteer training and activities with groups such as the Red Cross. She also organizes programmes herself, including sports training and other community services.

"I wasn't born in Hong Kong but I did spend my teen years here," says Ms Gurung, who originates from the scenic city of Pokhara, in central Nepal, which is known as a gateway to the Annapurna Circuit, a popular trail for trekking in the Himalayas.

The granddaughter of a Gurkha soldier of the British Army who was based in Hong Kong, Ms Gurung first started coming to Hong Kong for holidays to visit her parents when she was eight, moving here permanently four years later. Her grandfather has subsequently passed away, but Ms Gurung recalls chatting to him about his travel in Asia during his army days.

"My grandfather [Mahendra Bahadur Gurung] was based in the British army here in Fanling and my father was born here," she says, adding that she is proud of her Gurkha heritage. Ms Gurung lived with her family in Yuen Long and attended the Delia Memorial School (Broadway), where many of the pupils are of Pakistani, Nepalese or Indian heritage.

Both her parents have been keen to teach her about her Nepalese culture and Gurung heritage, she says. As a community, they mark Losar, the new year for the Gurung group, and a holiday that is also celebrated by other ethnic groups in Nepal.

"Nepal is a small country but with lots of ethnicities and multiculturalism so every family and caste has their own culture, traditions and practices, which is why different festivals are celebrated in the community here."

Prativa celebrates the festivals of Losar, Dashain and Tihar – the latter two are the main festivals across Nepal. "That's around

October and November and if you go to Nepal, it's quite beautiful," she says. But in Hong Kong there's not quite the same amount of space for these celebrations. "In Nepal we would have a big family gathering with blessings from the elders and plenty of lai see!" she says, using the Cantonese for small packets of "lucky" money, given as gifts, mostly for children.

Along with friends Elisa, Bithaya, Shresti and Anil, Prativa has produced radio programmes for the Nepalese community for RTHK's Community Involvement Broadcasting Service. Their first programme in 2016 was called "Role Model: Someone To Look Up To" where they informed and empowered Hong Kong Nepalese young people by interviewing role models within the Nepalese community. The second programme "Nepali Youth Roundtable" was a forum for Hong Kong Nepalese young people to talk about issues of importance to them and the community at large. "The topics ranged from culture, trends, aspirations to struggles and successes," says Prativa.

→ Prativa at Diamond Hill Park.

Sri Lankans – Travellers from the Tear Drop Nation

Sri Lankans-Travellers from the Tear Drop Nation

Sri Lanka, previously known as Ceylon, was part of British India. It gained its independence from Britain in February 1948. Today there are 2,000-3,000 Sri Lankans in Hong Kong. Some are doctors, professors, business people and other professionals; around 60 work for HSBC. Others are domestic helpers. Some came in the 1970s. Over 70 per cent have been in Hong Kong for more than 10 years; many have permanent residence and plan to stay.

They come from an island in the Indian Ocean – an island that is sometimes referred to as the tear drop beside India because of its shape. Its strategic location and deep natural harbours have helped it become a thriving centre of trade. This was true in the days of the ancient Silk Road that connected Asia to Europe and the Middle East as well as the more modern Silk Road promoted by China's President Xi Jinping. Its location and rich soil have attracted many invaders,

→ Worshippers pray during the Vesak Festival at Po Leung Kuk Lam Man Chan English Primary School in Hong Kong.

from the Indians and Portuguese to the Dutch and finally the British, who took hold of the island in 1815.

The British introduced large-scale tea and rubber plantations. The island became famous for its production and export of cinnamon, rubber and what is known as Ceylon tea. Today it is the world's second largest exporter of tea. The island won its independence in February 1948, taking the name of Sri Lanka.

This history has resulted in the island becoming home to many cultures, languages and religions. Its population includes Sinhalese,

Chapter 5 —— Sri Lankans – Travellers from the Tear Drop Nation

→ (Top) Venerable Sumiththa Thero prays at the
Sri Lankan Buddhist Cultural Centre.

→ (Bottom) A Sri Lankan pays her respects at the
Sri Lankan Buddhist Cultural Centre.

Tamils, Moors, Burghers, Malays, Chinese and aboriginal Vedda. The main religions are Buddhism, Hinduism, Islam and Christianity.

Prominent Sri Lankans in Hong Kong include the clinical and public health virologist Joseph Sriyal Malik Peiris, who became internationally recognized after his laboratory at the University of Hong Kong was the first to isolate the Severe Acute Respiratory Syndrome or SARS virus in 2003. An outbreak of SARS in southern China affected dozens of countries and resulted in the deaths of nearly 300 people in Hong Kong. Professor Malik Peiris had also been instrumental in the research into avian influenza, the first outbreak of which affected Hong Kong in 1997.

He was awarded Hong Kong's Silver Bauhinia Star in 2008 and became the first Sri Lankan to be elected a Fellow of the Royal Society of London in 2006. He was elected as a Foreign Member of the US National Academy of Science in 2017. He was also named one of the 10 "Science Stars of East Asia" by leading medical journal Nature in June 2018. Later in this chapter we also talk to Sri Lankan Hongkongers, writer and satirist Nury Vittachi and sports journalist Nazvi Careem.

Buddhists in Sri Lanka follow the Theravada tradition, a branch of

→ Buddha Puthun attends the Vesak Festival in Hong Kong.

the religion known for monastic discipline and one that literally means the "doctrine of the elders". Those living in Hong Kong celebrate the main Buddhist festivals, including the birthday of Buddha and the Poson Festival, which marks the arrival of the religion on the island. In past years, they did not have their own centre or temple so they celebrated these festivals in a Chinese or Thai Buddhist temple or in an open space. That changed in December 2016 with the establishment of the Sri Lankan Buddhist Cultural Centre in a residential building in the Prince Edward district. This was set up by the Venerable Sumiththa Thero, a Sri Lankan monk who arrived in Hong Kong in September 2015.

The following is based on a discussion with Venerable Sumiththa Thero. "I arrived in Hong Kong airport at midnight in September

2015. I knew no-one. I had the address of a Chinese Buddhist temple in Yuen Long. I gave it to a taxi driver and arrived there at 2:00 am. I was coming to do a one-year master's programme at the Centre of Buddhist Studies at Hong Kong University.

He was a residential monk at the Golden Temple in Dambulla, a World Heritage site 72 km north of Kandy in central Sri Lanka. That temple now has over 20 monks.

During his year of study, he gave talks at religious festivals; the community asked him to stay on. "I met Sri Lankan children who did not know of our culture. I started a class to teach them this culture and Buddhist principles because they have the right to know about their culture and religion."

So, after he completed the course, he set up a Sri Lankan Buddhist Cultural Centre, with contributions from 220 members, and rented space in a residential building in Prince Edward in December 2016.

In March 2017, they moved the centre to its current location, on the third floor of a mixed commercial/residential building in Sheung Heung Road, To Kwa Wan. The rent is HK$15,000 a month, modest for Hong Kong.

There they hold religious ceremonies and classes in meditation, Theravada Buddhist studies, ethics, Buddhist counseling and Sri Lankan cultural events. They organise annual blood donation campaigns with the Hong Kong Red Cross and distribute food – free of charge – at public gatherings.

"Each month we have an inter-faith dialogue with the imams from mosques, Sikh leaders and Christian scholars," he says.

"We now have around 700 members." Since the space is too small for large events, like celebrating the Buddha's birthday on May 27, they are hiring a hall at a nearby Po Leung Kuk Lam Man Chan English Primary School.

→ A lantern hangs at the Vesak Festival in Po Leung Kuk Lam Man Chan English Primary School in Hong Kong.

"We are open every day. As well as Sri Lankans, Chinese, Westerners, Indians and Malaysians come here to pray. Over 90 per cent come here and engage with pure hearts. Some have committed faults and mistakes and ask for guidance."

He decided that the community needed a proper temple, a permanent site to hold religious and cultural events.

"For the moment, we have registered as a society under the society ordinance of Hong Kong. We have applied for 20,000 square feet of land to the Home Affairs Bureau," he says. "They are processing our application. At their request, we have applied to register as a charitable organisation. Most suitable would be a site near a forest.

We need to build a hall for 300-400 people, plus a residential cottage, kitchen and space for traditional dancing and drumming. We would get architects and carpenters from home, perhaps for free. "Sri Lankan monks in Hong Kong could stay in the temple. I hope to include a small museum, to impart knowledge of Sri Lankan culture and history."

His aim is to have the temple up and running within five years and then return to Sri Lanka, to be replaced by another monk willing to take over. "It must be a permanent place. Then I can hand over. I cannot leave now, while we are in the middle of this project," he said. Sri Lankans practice the Theravada form of Buddhism while believers in Tibet and Mongolia follow the Vajrayana school and those in China, Taiwan, Korea, Vietnam and Japan follow the Mahayana school. As a Theravadan monk, Thero, who is 36, is not allowed to marry.

"Buddhism is atheist," he said. "The refuge is in you. You are the Master. You have all powers in you. You are your own saviour. You can destroy yourself or you can build a great noble character in you. If you behave badly, you will destroy yourself. If you behave in a good way, it will lead you and others to happiness. You can be a light to the world"

---

1.   Interview with Venerable Sumiththa Thero

2.   Interview with Nazvi Careem(13/5/2018)

3.   Interview with Nury Vittachi

4.   Multiculturalism in Action: Being Home: Bangladeshi and Sri Lankan Hongkongers – Program Director: Professor Siumi Maria Tam

Author, Satirist & Journalist

Nury Vittachi

→ Nury Vittachi is a keen observer of Asian life and its quirks.

With an English wife and three adopted Chinese children, Nury Vittachi's family is truly international. The Sri Lankan Hongkonger author of the bestselling The Feng Shui Detective series, who also co-founded the Hong Kong International Literary Festival, was born in Colombo in 1958.

"I originate from Sri Lanka, it was called Ceylon in those days. I was born there in 1958, which is also the exact time the Sinhalese-Tamil war started," says Mr Vittachi. "I was born in Colombo. There's only one big city in Sri Lanka basically so we're all born in Colombo hospitals. My father had a very long connection with Hong Kong though. So in my 20s I got married and we came here on honeymoon and never left."

Mr Vittachi's father was an award-winning journalist and one of the first investigative journalists in Asia. When the Sri Lankan war broke out, the prime minister ordered journalists not to write about it. But "my father thought this was absurd. So my father, who was known as Tarzie Vittachi, wrote a book about the Sri Lankan war, and smuggled it out of the country. "

While the world came to know about the war in Sri Lanka, it also led to Mr Vittachi and his family having to leave Sri Lanka, although they have been back subsequently. His father would later be awarded the Ramon Magsaysay Award, equivalent to an Asian Nobel prize, for his courageous journalism.

Nury Vittachi was educated in England, but hankered to come back to Southeast Asia. He and his wife came to Hong Kong and he recalls the feel of the humid air on his face as he left the plane, "and I remember thinking this is what air is supposed to feel like. I'm home, I'm really home."
While the Sri Lankan community is small in Hong Kong, Mr Vittachi says informal attempts are made to create societies for Sri Lankan culture. "There was a big boost when the Sri Lankan helpers started to arrive. There have been attempts at setting up Sri Lankan societies, but all very informal."

He also cooks Sri Lankan food at home, which is loved by his children. While he feels the food is similar to Indian, "every part of South Asia has a different twist".

"In Sri Lanka we use a lot of coconut milk. It's hot, but it's also tasty. I mean there's two types of hopper. There's the crisp pancake with an egg in the middle. There's also a noodle-based hopper like noodles that have been left out too long and have formed into a plate – which sounds disgusting but it's actually very nice.

"I eat a lot of white curry fish. White means not spicy. But it's all comparative, so it will still blow some people's heads off. White fish curries are used in the mornings, but a lot of Westerners can't abide the idea of eating a hot curry in the morning."

For many years, Mr Vittachi wrote the satirical Lai See column at the *South China Morning Post*, which not only led to plenty of enthused reader input and suggestions but also a number of legal writs. "I regarded them as badges of honour," he says. These days, Mr Vittachi usually works on three books simultaneously – a non-fiction book, "I've always been very interested in science", a novel and also a children's book.

"My father was a Muslim, my mother was Buddhist, and my wife's Christian, so I've kind of got the set," he says. "When we adopted three Chinese kids, we were told bring them up in their own culture. So technically they should be Taoists. I just need one of them to marry a Jew, then we really have all the biggies."

As well as cooking Sri Lankan savoury food at home, Mr Vittachi enjoys the Sri Lankan puddings.

"There are a lot of lovely Sri Lankan desserts," he says. "And one dessert is called love cake and the recipe was stolen from the Europeans, the Dutch, I think. Various European nations colonized Sri Lanka and we kept bits of recipes from each of them. And one we stole was the love cake, which is a very moist cake so it's very dense and rich and moist and honey-flavoured and it just melts in your mouth. It's one of those things that eventually will go international because it's so calorific and evil. It really fits the modern appetite."

Many of Mr Vittachi's newspaper columns and books over the years have included observations of Asian life and its quirks. He's also a keen observer of the mix of languages that occur in every day speech and life in this region.

"One of the funny things is that there is a whole subgroup of language which Chinese in Hong Kong assume is English and English speakers assume is Chinese. But they come from mostly from South Asian travellers. So Indian, Malay Indian, Islamic groups and so on," he says.

→ Nury Vittachi cooks Sri Lankan food at home
for his family.

So here are some examples:
Catty – used as a measure, often for vegetables. The word is neither Chinese nor English, but in fact Malay.

"Shroff is another one," says Mr Vittachi. "It means cashier in one of the Indian languages." Shroff was first used back in the 16th century in the British East Indies as a word for cashier or banker.

"Congee is also interesting," he says, "because it sounds so Chinese to English speakers but is originally Dravidian," so a language family spoken mainly in southern India.

"Coolie conjures images of porters wearing those conical straw hats, but it probably comes from kuli, a Hindi term meaning hired servant," he says. It has also been associated with the Urdu word for slave.

"What could be more Chinese than palanquin," says Mr Vittachi of the covered box, where one passenger is carried on horizontal poles by four to eight bearers. But the word comes from the Sanskrit "palyanka" meaning bed or couch.
"I love these as examples because they show the invisibility of the South Asian community. We're there but we're not there," he says.

And then there's the Bund in Shanghai. It's a Hindi word for water enclosure, he says. "So the early residents for the river Pu were Chinese; the colonialists setting up the infrastructure were British, but the workers pulling the barges along the river bank were Indian. So it was the Indian workers who ended up naming it. I like that image because it shows the South Asian role of the middleman in Asia holding the east and west together."

Sports Journalist

Nazvi Careem

→ Sports writer Nazvi Careem has followed his father, Nicky, into a career in journalism.

Nazvi Careem is an independent sports writer, whose articles can often be seen in the *South China Morning Post* newspaper. The veteran journalist came to Hong Kong from Sri Lanka in 1968 at the age of two. "I was born in Colombo, but I'd consider myself from Galle [further south along the Sri Lankan coast]. I consider Hong Kong to be my home," he says. "Sri Lanka is still very close to my heart. I used to go there for holidays regularly and have relatives there. So Sri Lanka is still a big part of my life. "

Mr Careem's grandfather came to Hong Kong in the 1950s. He was followed by his son – and Nazvi's father – Nicky, who was the first in the family to be bitten by the journalism bug. "My dad was actually in the jewellery business initially," says Nazvi Careem. "He was working for Duty Free and at that time they had an office in Tsim Sha Tsui. So basically he was here but went to Sir Lanka for an arranged marriage. He then returned to Hong Kong and when he felt we were old enough he brought us over here. Hong Kong was always going to be our home."

After jewellery, Nicky Careem turned to his real love – journalism – and worked for years at a variety of publications in the territory, including the Hong Kong Standard newspaper, the *South China Morning Post* and also a magazine in the 1980s called China Sources.

"He really liked that job," says his sports writer son, "because he got to travel to China quite often. [China's paramount leader] Deng Xiaoping was just opening up China to the world and my father was a bit of a Sinophile." Mr Careem relates how his father told him that being brown-skinned made him quite the novelty on the mainland at that time. "As a brown man, he would be surrounded by people."

Within the home, Nazvi, a father of seven, says it was the food that exemplified the family's "Sri Lankan-ness". "We had some close relatives also living in Tsim Sha Tsui, so they would come to us and us to them. I would say our 'Sri Lankan-ness was about 20 per cent of our lifestyle here. It was there and it was strong but it wasn't an overriding lifestyle, I would say."

Mr Careem would go on to attend two English Schools Foundation schools – Beacon Hill and King George V School, where he thrived on team sports, becoming the school's hockey team captain, as were both his cousin and brother in other years.

"My brother and my cousin went on to join the 'Hong Kong Schoolboys", he says, which was a Hong Kong national hockey team for school-aged boys.

Mr Careem says his mother, Haleema Dheen, is a superb baker. So he grew up on great Sri Lankan dishes but also European cakes and desserts. "My mum was a cake maker and she even appeared on the television once making cakes. Her desserts were colonially based – biscuit and bread puddings, which we loved."

She would later use her Sri Lankan culinary skills to open the famous Club Sri Lanka on Wyndham Street, with all you could eat buffets, which she had until the family left in 2000. "At home we would have Sri Lankan chicken curry, which I love. My father always used to get irritated when people mixed up Indian and Sri Lankan food. He felt that was like saying Italian and French food are the same.

"We would also have the traditional Sri Lankan hoppers, like roti but bowl shaped with an egg in the middle. My mum would also make string hoppers that look like noodles and delicious desserts made with palm sugar from the coconut trees."

As a Sri Lankan Muslim, Mr Careem says he doesn't follow all the Sri Lankan festivals, but he observes Ramadan and does that in a Sri Lankan way. On the first night of Ramadan he says, his mother would cook up a feast of egg curry, dhal, chicken and potato curry among other dishes.

Many of his schoolmates didn't know where Sri Lanka was, he says. "I remember lying about my birthday once," he says. "Everyone else was seven and I wasn't seven yet. Apparently it was my country's birthday that day, so Mrs Morton, my teacher, used it as an opportunity for everyone to learn about the country. And that's when I learned that Sri Lanka was famous for tea."

→ Nazvi Careem was a hockey team captain at King George V School, as were his brother and cousin.

Textiles, Bengali Culture and Islam

Textiles, Bengali Culture and Islam

The country that is now Bangladesh was once part of British India. The Partition of India in 1947 granted the territory that is now Bangladesh to Pakistan, but after a bitter nine-month war in 1971, Bangladesh won its independence. Independence came at a high cost – some three million lives were lost.

Today there are 600 Bangladeshi families in Hong Kong, or a total of about 1,500 people, according to some estimates. Most Bangladeshis in Hong Kong are Muslims while a small number are Hindu or Buddhist. Muslims in Hong Kong generally observe the main Muslim festivals, such as Eid-at-Fitr (Festival of Breaking the Fast), gathering at the local mosques for morning prayers and then visiting each other's homes. They gather every Friday for prayers at the city's mosques and listen to the sermon of the imam. Hindu Bangladeshis pray with other Hindus from west Bengal, which is part of India.

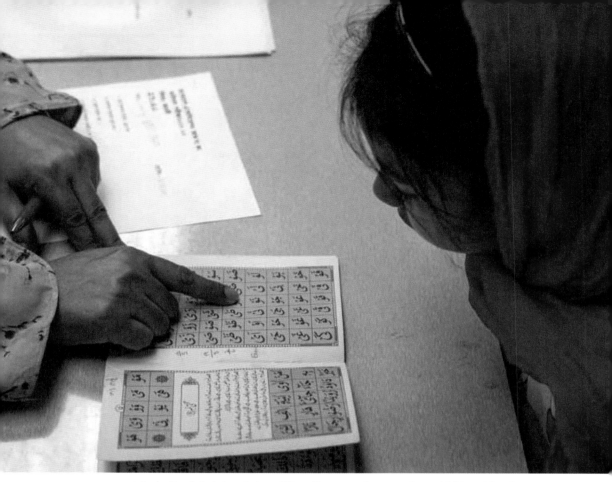

→ At the Bangladesh Association of Hong Kong, a teacher supervises a child in reciting the Bengali language during the final examination of a weekend school.

For Bengali Hindus, the most important festival of the year is Durga Puja, which is celebrated in September or October. It lasts for several days and involves elaborate temple and stage decorations, recitations of scripture, performances and processions. Each year the Bengali Hindu community in the territory invites a priest from India to lead the religious ceremonies at Durga Puja.

Ikram Ahmed Khan, president of the Bangladesh Chamber of Commerce & Industry Hong Kong, says the first Bangladeshi came to Hong Kong in 1964 – even before the creation of Bangladesh as an independent country. "Before independence in 1971, it was not

Chapter 6 —— Textiles, Bengali Culture and Islam

→ (From Left to right) Ikram Ahmed Khan and his business partners, Mohammed Ali Pasha and M. Kamal A. Pasha. Khan came to Hong Kong with his family in 1990.

easy for us to get passports. In 1976, the Bangladesh Consulate was set up here. We could obtain three-month landing visas. But most Bangladeshi migrants chose to go to English-speaking countries in Europe and North America," he says.

Bangladesh faced many difficulties in its early years. It had no foreign reserves, because Pakistan did not share its wealth after the separation. Between March and December 1974, the county was hit by a famine, and some estimates put the death toll at 1.5 million. On August 15, 1975, a group of soldiers and senior officers assassinated Sheikh Mujibur Rahman, the president and "Bangabandhu" – the Father of the Nation. The military seized power, leading to a prolonged period of political and economic instability. Another blow was the global trend towards using plastics as a wrapping material –

replacing jute, one of the most important cash crops of Bangladesh. The country produced 80 per cent of the global output of jute in 1947-48 and still is the world's second largest producer today.

Khan said that all these factors triggered economic migration from the country in the 1980s. "Bangladeshis started to come to Hong Kong in larger numbers in the late 1980s," says Khan, who came with his family in 1990. "They came to work for Bangladesh firms in the garment industry, to find buyers for their goods or source fabrics and other materials from China." Bangladesh is one of the world's largest producers of garments; in 2017, garments accounted for more than 80 per cent of the country's total exports of US$25 billion. "Our nationals here work in garment firms, banks, shipping companies and as government interpreters. Everyone is staying for the long term. Most have Hong Kong Chinese passports. They go back to Bangladesh for business and for summer holidays." There are also several hundred domestic maids from Bangladesh; the government target is to recruit 10,000.

Khan was full of praise for the business environment in Hong Kong. "It is one of the friendliest places in the world for a business visa. InvestHK provides good support to all investors. A company secretary can set up a company in one day. Since the handover, I see zero interference by the central government; it sees the city as a source of growth. I tell my friends to invest here. Since 1997, it has become safer thank to control of triads by the central government. Before the handover, triads used to steal cars and rob shops but no more since the handover. No-one has ever asked me for protection money," he says.

"Bangladesh is becoming the second Dongguan, a Chinese manufacturing centre, due to the Belt & Road initiative of the central government," he adds, referring to China's programme to boost infrastructure investment in a number of strategically important countries and thereby enhance trade.

"Since the visit to Bangladesh by (Chinese) President Xi Jinping in

Chapter 6 —— Textiles, Bengali Culture and Islam

2016, about US$40 billion has been allocated to finance various projects in Bangladesh. The Bangladesh government should make Mandarin mandatory in schools. We have Bangladesh boys here with Hong Kong passports and knowledge of Mandarin; Chinese firms can send them to work in their offices or in factories in Bangladesh. They can regard them as more reliable because they have roots and a home in Hong Kong."

He said that there was also no sign of Islamophobia in Hong Kong. "There is more freedom for us as Muslims here. We have freedom of speech and freedom to perform religious duties – the same as for other religions and ethnic minorities. The Hong Kong government has recently approved two new mosques, in Yau Ma Tei and Sheung Shui, while some countries do not approve building new mosques.

"We do not feel apart from Bangladesh. We communicate with Bangladesh on a daily basis. There is no identity crisis for the first generation, like me and my wife," he says, though he suggests that could change. "This second generation speaks Bengali, but they do not read or write it. That means they are not comfortable in Bangladesh; how can they manage local people? They cannot read documents or text messages in Bengali.

"The culture shock is coming and will dilute ethnicity. Young Bangladeshi people here marry Chinese and British. Hong Kong people have no time for discrimination. They are too busy. Hong Kong men are genetically not aggressive. Our women never complain of being stared at or threatened. Racial discrimination is very low."

Khan said that Hong Kong had many advantages – an excellent business environment, a reliable legal system and good security, no prejudice against non-Chinese or any particular religion and a strong public health system. Its downsides are high costs, particularly housing and education. "The education system here is not student-friendly and forward-looking. There is too much homework and pressure; teachers are overworked and bully students.

"Bangladesh parents choose private schools, which cost up to HK$100,000 per year. The living costs are so high that young

Bangladeshis prefer to live in Guangzhou, Kunming or Shanghai. No new young ones are coming, except students who win scholarships. A nephew of mine won a scholarship in civil engineering from Hong Kong University; he is a star student and has been given a job at Arup & Partners. We hope a new breed of talent will come and be given quicker visas. The Hong Kong government wants to encourage IT specialists, in which Bangladesh is very strong. I hope it brings in Bangladesh talent."

Is it hard to be a pious Muslim and observe Ramadan? "It is not difficult. You can pray at sunrise and at lunchtime. In the afternoon, you can pray in your office for a few minutes. I keep a prayer mat in my office." Ramadan lasts for one month; between sunrise and sunset, an observant Muslim must not eat or drink, have sexual

→ The young generation of Bangladeshis have a choice of career. Two students attend the weekend school at the Bangladesh Association of Hong Kong.

Chapter 6 —— Textiles, Bengali Culture and Islam

relations or engage in sinful behavior. "Ramadan is most welcome. I feel guilty because I have air conditioning and a cook to make our food. Other Muslim brothers are working outside in the hot sun. The more difficult it is, the more blessings he will obtain. God will love those with more purity."

Is it hard to find halal food? "Hong Kong is behind other places in this respect. Halal food is a nearly one-trillion-dollar business in the world. But halal food is hard to find here. Some hotels, like the Sheraton, Conrad and Holiday Inn, have halal menus if you order in advance. Less than five per cent of Hong Kong's tourists are from Muslim countries; it could be 15 per cent, if halal food was more readily available and Muslims felt more welcome." An observant Muslim may not drink alcohol, which can be a problem for a businessman like Khan who must often attend social events and banquets. "In Japan, you can find alcohol-free beer everywhere, as well as halal champagne. They will provide halal glasses that have never been mixed with alcohol. This is missing in Hong Kong. When I am frank and honest about this, people do not object; they respect my standards."

→ *Bangladesh Association*

In October 2003, with the support of its expatriates here, the Bangladesh Association of Hong Kong was established. Its aim is to promote Bangladeshi unity, culture and language. It provides a venue for Bangladeshi children to learn Bengali, their mother tongue, which is not taught in local schools or institutions. The association also aims to promote Southeast Asian culture and serve as a bridge for relations with other cultures. The centre provides information about Bangladeshi culture – from language to music and dance. It promotes reading and writing of basic Bengali, Arabic and other languages. "This will allow us to practise and strengthen our own culture and enhance our cultural heritage, while we are in different cultural environment," the centre says on its website. It has one supervisor, six teachers and 30 students enrolled in its Bengali and Arabic language classes. Children also learn Bengali songs and dances

→ Lubna Farhin, supervisor of the weekend school, conducts a final examination for students at the Bangladesh Association of Hong Kong.

which they perform at special festivals. The centre organises cricket and badminton tournaments and organises celebrations for National Day, Bengali New Year, the Eid al-Fitr festival and Buddha's birthday, to keep cultural and religious traditions alive.

The Bangladesh government has a consulate-general for Hong Kong and Macau, staffed by a diplomat from its Foreign Ministry, Mohammad Sarwar Mahmood. He told an investment seminar in 2018 that there were 150 Bangladeshi companies in Hong Kong, focusing on garments, leather, computer software and pharmaceuticals. Three Bangladesh banks have operations here. "Hong Kong is a super-connector" for his country, he said, in facilitating its trade and finance. "It is a major financial centre as well as a crucial sourcing and distribution hub in Asia and a gateway to global trade.

Chapter 6 —— Textiles, Bengali Culture and Islam

Historically, Hong Kong is an active business partner of Bangladesh." Hong Kong was the seventh largest foreign investor in Bangladesh, with cumulative direct investment of US$769 million as of the end of September 2017. In 2017, bilateral trade was US$1.7 billion.

In 2017, Bangladesh's GDP reached US$250 billion, ranking it 44th in the world; by 2030, it aims to reach 28th position. Its GDP in 2017 was up 150 per cent from the 2009 level of US$100 billion. China has invested US$40 billion in Bangladesh, mostly in large infrastructure projects, as part of its Belt and Road initiative. As of the end of September 2017, cumulative mainland Chinese investment in the country was US$283.77 billion.

→ *Chamber of Commerce*

The Bangladesh Chamber of Commerce & Industry Hong Kong was

→ Mr. Khan being interviewed by the Media at a Chamber event.

set up as a business support group in March 2017. It has 45 member firms and 14 associate members. It aims to build and reinforce ties between Bangladesh and Hong Kong, Macau and China by establishing and maintaining effective partnerships with businesses, governments, other business chambers and stakeholder agencies. It also aims to initiate, support or oppose legislation or other policies in trade, commerce, shipping and manufacturing which affect Bangladesh, Hong Kong and China. It is a not-for-profit organisation which utilises membership fees and other income to provide support and resources to businesses and institutions across Hong Kong and China that wish to trade with Bangladesh.

Khan, the chamber president, said that in recent years, the social, political and business links among Bangladesh, Hong Kong, Macau and China have deepened significantly. "The business-friendly environment and competitive corporate tax structure has encouraged many Bangladeshi entrepreneurs to establish successful businesses in Hong Kong. At the same time, Bangladesh has become one of Asia's most investment-friendly countries, and its low-cost labour has attracted many companies from Hong Kong, Macau and China to invest in Bangladesh."

Mr. Khan is also the managing director of Shun Shing Group International, (www.ssgil.com), an international trade and investment company that produces, markets and transports cement and related raw materials as well as coal to global customers. It also has packaging and stevedoring operations. Founded in 1988 and headquartered in Hong Kong, it has over 2,000 employees of 18 nationalities in offices in Asia and the Middle East.

1.   Interview with Ikram Ahmed Khan

Chapter 6 —— Textiles, Bengali Culture and Islam

Textiles and Charity

Dewan *Saiful Alam Masud*

→ Dewan Masud with his wife, Umme Kulsom Bonnie, right, and two daughters, Zareen Tasnim Alam and Simine Tasnim Alam.

Dewan Saiful Alam Masud has lived in Hong Kong for more than 25 years. The father of two daughters runs a company that makes clothes in Bangladesh. But Mr Masud also does a huge amount of volunteer work that has seen him recognized both by NGOs and the Hong Kong government alike.

Born near the historic city of Brahmanbaria in Bangladesh, Mr Masud started working for a textile firm there after graduating. The company then posted him to Hong Kong in February 1993. It took him a few months to settle into Hong Kong life – there were no Bangladeshi restaurants, he was missing his family. Hong Kong felt small and expensive.

"But gradually I adjusted," he says. "Slowly I started eating Chinese food. I think this is normal for everyone as they adjust."
These days he eats plenty of Bangladeshi food with his wife, Umme Kulsum Bonnie, and two daughters, Simine Tasnim Alam, 16, and Zareen Tasnim Alam, 14. But he also finds that his daughters – as two born and bred Hongkongers – have developed tastes for Japanese, Chinese and other cuisines, so food at home has become more "fusion".

"I like typical Bangladeshi food, but I'm a little overweight – so used to enjoying biryani. Bangladeshis are also into sweet meats, so I need to watch the calories. Bangladesh is a country full of rivers, so we enjoy different kinds of river fish either made into curry or fried."

His daughters attend English Schools Foundation schools, and are both now at King George V School in Ho Man Tin. Mr Masud is keen to maintain their Bangladeshi heritage, the "culture from their parents and grandparents, but I appreciate that living here means it's mixing up a bit."

Mr Masud has done two stints as president of the Bangladeshi Association of Hong Kong. He also assists with weekend activities for Bangladeshi children, where they learn music and dance, as well as other aspects of their culture. They also learn Arabic to read the Muslim holy book, the Quran, as 85 per cent of the Bangladeshi population here is Muslim.

"It's a weekend school every Saturday. Our children learn how to do folk dances and sing Bengali songs. We also bring in some renowned artists to perform. These have included singers Runa Laila and Sabina Yasmin.

At home, Mr Masud's daughters speak English and Bengali. "Of course, there's a lot of pressure on our children to learn different languages," he says. "At school they also learn Mandarin and one European language."

While he came out to Hong Kong with a firm, Mr Masud has long since been self-employed running a textile business. He has been chief executive of the DSA International Company in Hong Kong and Dhaka since 1999. He says most of the Bangladeshi community here are involved in textiles. "There are 5,000 textile factories in Bangladesh making clothes," he says. "They need materials imported from China including fabrics, buttons and zippers. The clothes are then sewn in Bangladesh and exported to the United States and Europe. Bangladesh is the second largest clothing exporter after China."

Mr Masud feels Bangladesh is a country that should be explored more by tourists. "I think because it is majority Muslim and therefore a little bit conservative in terms of alcoholic drinks, people like to go to other places," he says. But once they get out of Dhaka, which is crowded and full of traffic, he says, they can discover the beauty of his home country – such as Cox's Bazaar, the longest, uninterrupted natural beach in the world. Then there are the tea gardens to visit, he says. Britain's East India Company initiated the tea trade in Chittagong in 1840, so there is a long heritage.

Mr Masud was named on the non-governmental organisation, the Zubin Foundation's, diversity list for 2017 for his work with non-ethnic Chinese minorities. He is also active with other NGOs and was awarded the Chief Executive's Commendation for Community Service in 2013.

→ Dewan Masud and his family at a social occasion.

From Momos to Masala – South Asian Food in Hong Kong

From Momos to Masala-South Asian Food in Hong Kong

One important legacy of the long history of South Asians in Hong Kong is the rich and varied cuisine they have brought with them. According to some estimates, they own or manage as much as 10 per cent of all restaurants in the city.

The cuisines of South Asia are as diverse as the people, religions and languages of the region. They include the rich and buttery flavour of the basmati rice of the Punjab in Northwest India. Punjab is one of India's biggest producers of dairy products – so these form an important part of the cuisine.

India has more than 300 million vegetarians – more than the rest of the world put together. In the western state of Rajasthan, the proportion is 75 per cent, the highest in the country. This has produced an abundant vegetarian and vegan cuisine, which can be

→ Chef Kamal Kishore makes garlic naan at Gaylord Indian Restaurant.

found on the streets of Hong Kong. Their restaurants offer many delicious varieties of vegetables, beans and fruit, as well as thali, masala dosa, vindaloo, tiffin and gulab jamun. To cater for the widest choice, restaurants offer meat, vegetarian and vegan options.
So, on your travels, do not be shy. Try something new and unknown. Take home with you the tastes of Telugu and Tamil Nadu.

Hong Kong also offers plenty of halal options including Pakistani, Indian and Bangladeshi food. There's also a couple of Sri Lankan restaurants, one offering authentic Sri Lankan street food in Sheung Wan.

→ Saunf, a mix of fennel seeds used to refresh the mouth after meals.

Prices of South Asian food are generally very reasonable compared to other cuisines. A main dish is usually under HK$100 and plenty of smaller dishes are around the HK$40 mark. Head into the warren of Chungking Mansions on Nathan Road in Kowloon and there's plenty of snacks including samosas, naan, roti and that taste great but won't put a dent in your pocket. There are numerous options for a birthday party or business lunch. Tsim Sha Tsui is a really great centre for Indian food, but there are alternatives throughout Hong Kong on Hong Kong Island, Kowloon and in the New Territories.

Enjoy!

→ *Gaylord Indian Restaurant*

At the top of Ashley Road in Tsim Sha Tsui there's Hong Kong's oldest Indian restaurant, the Gaylord, established in 1972 by businessman O.P. Seth. A few years later the Gaylord Indian Restaurant was bought by the Harilela Restaurant Group. Rajeev Bhasin was brought in from Delhi to oversee the operation in 1991. Mr Bhasin later teamed up with a group of other investors and formed the Mayfare Group which eventually took over the iconic restaurant. Now he is the group's managing director, and he has been looking after Gaylord and the other establishments in the group's portfolio.

"I've been in Hong Kong for almost 30 years," he says. "I've seen [last Hong Kong governor] Chris Patten here, lots of Bollywood stars and the god of cricket Sachin Tendulkar. He was back here in 1995, representing India at the Hong Kong Sixes here. And the whole team was invited to our restaurant. And I have a hat from him which is signed."

Gaylord provides primarily North Indian fare. The restaurant also offers other regional specials and dishes reflecting ingredients of the changing seasons.

Many customers have been coming for several generations, says Mr Bhasin, whose Mayfare Group took over Gaylord in 2014. "We have a group of Indian couples who have been coming two to three Saturdays a month since we opened in 1972."

The name Gaylord is meant to convey a sense of "Happy God". A statue of Lord Shiva, the most powerful god in the Hindu pantheon, stands at the front to welcome arriving guests. "Any Harilela businesses you go you will see the statue of Lord Shiva – you will see it in the Hollywood Inn Golden Mile and at their other international businesses. And we have Shiva at the entrance. So Shiva sees anyone coming into the entrance and blesses them."

→ A statue of Lord Shiva stands at the front of Gaylord Indian Restaurant to welcome arriving guests.

While Gaylord provides seasonal fare, their main menu consists of North Indian signature items. These include samosas, chicken tandoori, lamb kebabs, barbecued prawns, the spinach and cheese, cauliflower and potato- the aloo gobi, as well as buttered chicken, and chicken tikka masala.

"I think when people come out to eat they are looking for something special," says Mr Bhasin. "No one is going to have a tandoori oven in a Hong Kong home, so they can't get the tandoori chicken at home, they can't have a naan at home. Not in a charcoal oven. Saag paneer [spinach with Indian cheese] is too much trouble to make at home."

Eating habits have changed over the years, he says. Indian restaurants would often be famed in Hong Kong for all you can eat buffets. But while buffet style eating is still available, the emphasis is more on healthy eating while staying true to the Indian origins. So customers can have tapas style Indian dishes, so that they have a taste of everything without the meal sizes being too large. In the same way, says Mr Bhasin, in a more health-conscious society, they try to reduce the level of oil in the food, while retaining all the flavour.

"We do a simple yellow lentils, the barbecue is always healthy. Indian and Middle Eastern are the only cuisines where the bread is cooked to order. We can cook a naan on the charcoal oven in 20 seconds in front of you. That's the joy of this cuisine.

"The barbecue is chargrilled – the flavour that you can get from a tandoor – the clay oven is amazing. So you have this lovely smoky smell, also with the bread. You don't have that in a bakery – they often add emulsifiers and other chemicals. We add yeast, but our yeast is yoghurt."

Growing up in Delhi, Mr Bhasin was introduced to all the regional cuisines by his mother, who would also cook depending on changing seasons – winter, summer, monsoon. The various colonizers of India over the centuries, including the Portuguese, he says, have had an influence on the food.

There are also around 200 varieties of mango to choose from in India, so a simple but delicious drink in the heat is what is called Milkshake Mango that is dipped into iced water. Then you cut off the top of the Dussehri Mango, dubbed the King of Mangoes, and drink the lovely mango inside. It's a soft green mango that is available in north India around May and June. Then there's also the Alfonso mango from the West.

"During the summer there is a lot of rose-flavoured drinks, a lot of biryanis, [a South Asian spicy rice dish], a lot of barbequed mangoes. Like roasted corn on the cob, we also roast the mangoes. Grilled barbecue mangoes.

Through this you can also create a kind of fruit chaat – so a mixture of bits and pieces on one plate, including grilled pineapple.

Gaylord's resident musician and singer Mushtaq Hassan recently arrived from Delhi. He is actually from a well known family of classical musicians in Delhi, but his restaurant repertoire is a mix of Bollywood hits, Sufi songs and customer requests.

"We have chef who has been working for 25 years and a chef who is 65 and has just retired, who used to work in the tandoor – people didn't need to order. The guests would make eye contact with him and the naan would then be served for them when they come to the table," says Mr Bhasin.

→ A pile of poppadoms.

→ *Halal restaurants*

Jashan on Hollywood Road and the Jo Jo restaurants are culinary fixtures in Hong Kong – the latter started out more than 30 years ago. They provide halal certified food with signature dishes from across South Asia. The restaurants are among seven run by the Uppal Hospitality Group. They were founded by Kuldip Singh Uppal, the group's executive director, who began serving food for his father's restaurant Jo Jo Mess back in the mid-1980s. As well as running these seven restaurants, the group also supplies airline Cathay Pacific Airways with all its halal and vegetarian cuisine.

Mr Uppal's father, Tarsem Singh Uppal, served in Hong Kong's police force under the British on Stonecutters Island, before opening Jo Jo Mess in Wan Chai in 1985, now Jo Jo Indian Cuisine. Mr Uppal would help out serving customers at the restaurant, with his brother Sukwinder and mother cooking in the kitchen. He came with his brother to Hong Kong in 1982 from Jalandhar in Punjab state.

Mr Uppal earlier told *South China Morning Post* senior writer Bernice Chan of 18-hour days in the early years – holding down day jobs and then working at the restaurant in the evenings. It was a gruelling start. Now more than three decades on, Mr Uppal tells of how he has recently embarked on a culinary journey to "showcase various geographical and cultural influences on Indian food by focusing on the 'Grand Trunk Road', which features food from Afghanistan to Bangladesh".

So the Jo Jo menu includes dhansak, a Parsee dish of lamb and lentils, and a Bengali spicy fish stew, as well as dishes from Iran and Afghanistan.

Over on Hollywood Road, Jashan was opened in 2003 and has grown to become the go-to venue for iftar meals at the end of the fasting day during Ramadan. It also supplies the major mosques for social occasions. Tariq or Terry Mahmood is Mr Uppal's operation director and was brought by him from Dubai to head Jashan 15 years ago.

→ Jashan Celebrating Indian Cuisine on Hollywood Road.

"I was born in Pakistan and then went with my parents to Dubai," he says. "I went to school and on to management school there. Later I joined J W Marriott hotels and then Sheraton Hotels Dubai."

"There are so many consulates here," he says. As a halal-certified restaurant, staff from the Malaysian, Indonesian, UAE and Saudi Arabian consulates are among Jashan's regular clients. Jashan has a wide menu of Indian, Pakistani and Bangladeshi dishes, and the quality of the food saw Jashan become the first Indian restaurant in Hong Kong recognized in the Michelin Guide for 2013.

Chef Anil Datt also won the Hong Kong award for Outstanding Quality Tourism Services 2017.

→ Jo jo Indian Cuisine on Lockhart Road.

"We really focus on the food quality," says Mr Mahmood. "All the ingredients come from India, but our chef makes the recipes here. We don't use any MSG, and we try to keep the food light and not too heavy."

Among the halal signature dishes are the Kashmiri lamb curry, the mixed grill and the Hydrabadi lamb biryani. Jashan also offers other Pakistani dishes including kadai chicken and Peshawar chapli kebab. (Kadai is a two-handled wok).

For those who like things a bit spicier, Mr Mahmood suggests the Goan lamb vindaloo. Another signature dish is the Lucknowi nihari, a slow-cooked stew with lamb shank, left to marinate for one day before being cooked for at least three hours.

So what does halal mean in terms of food? It's a dietary standard for Muslims as prescribed by the Koran. "So the meat has to be slaughtered in a certain way," says Mr Mahmood. "We have Australian and New Zealand chicken, also lamb, and we have certification from Incorporated Trustees of Islamic Community Fund of Hong Kong that is 100 per cent halal. And they come and do spot checks. "

Jashan also serves Delhi style street food, including chaat, mini-bite items. There are the dahi poori a round, hollow fried crisp dough filled with tamarind chutney, chili, potato, onion, chaat masala and chickpeas.

Jashan also serves the famed golgappa shots – short drinks, as the name suggests that can be a mix of fruit juice, cumin seeds, chopped basil and mint.

Mr Mahmood says Jashan is also offering chicken tikka samosas. "Nobody else in Hong Kong offers that, this is the first time we are introducing it," he says.

For Diwali festive occasions, Jashan also offers homemade fresh sweets, that banks and other business clients buy for their customers in gift boxes as well as families and other customers. These include injeer burfi, kaju katli, doda burfi, boondi ladoo and almond burfi, an Indian delicacy traditionally made of milk, sugar and cardamom powder and a special fixture during festivals and celebrations.

→ Jo jo Indian Cuisine's Jujeh Kebab. Chunks of chicken that have been marinated and then grilled for this popular Iranian dish.

Here are the addresses for the halal restaurants mentioned above and some other choices.

≡ **Jashan Celebrating Indian Cuisine**
  *Serves Mega Buffet Lunch and Sunday Brunch and A La Carte Dinner
  Amber Lodge, 23 Hollywood Rd, Central
  Tel: 3105 5300, 92014775

≡ **Jo Jo Indian Cuisine**
  David House, 37-39 Lockhart Rd, Wan Chai
  Tel: 2527 3776

Other South Asian-style halal restaurant options include:

≡ **Aladin Mess**
  2/F, 60 Russell Street,
  Causeway Bay
  Tel: 2808 0250

≡ **Shaffi's Indian Restaurant**
  G/F, 14 Fau Tsoi Street,
  Yuen Long
  Tel:2476 7885
  (Shaffi's started out serving British troops Indian food in the 1970s and still remains very popular with customers for its curries.)

≡ **Bombay Dreams**
  77 Wyndham St, Central
  Tel: 2971 0001

→ *South Indian Vegetarian Options*

South Indian food is not wholly vegetarian, although a good proportion of it is. In the far south in Tamil Nadu, among other regions, there are plenty of dishes to be had with mutton and chicken. But for the purposes of this review and to cater to lacto vegetarians, vegans and Jains, the choices here are for vegetarian restaurants in Hong Kong which serve predominantly South Indian fare, although some also have North Indian dishes on their menu.

Say to anyone, "Indian vegetarian" in Hong Kong and Woodlands International Restaurant is top of the list. This straightforward restaurant in Tsim Sha Tsui has been serving up South Indian vegetarian fare since 1981. And a big plus is that it's Indian food

→ Palak paneer, cottage cheese in a spinach gravy.

for Hong Kong Indians who make up a large share of the clientele. So it's the real deal. The restaurant has been cited on Trip Advisor as having "the best dosas I have tasted outside India". Also try the delicious thali – a selection of Indian meals served up on a platter.

Sangeetha Restaurant also in Tsim Sha Tsui is part of a chain, with its headquarters and origins in Chennai in India. It serves both South and North Indian food, but specializes in South Indian cuisine derived from a traditional Udupi and Chettinad style of cooking. Udupi cuisine comprises dishes made primarily from grains, beans, vegetables and fruits. Chettinad cuisine originates from Tamil Nadu and uses a variety of spices, and the dishes are put together with fresh ground masalas. In the food on offer at Sangeetha are authentic Indian recipes influenced by Mughal and Chinese cuisine.

→ Mirchi kebabs made with green chillis.

Sangeetha's menu has more than 20 types of dosa and a medley of uthappam, the thick pancake with ingredients cooked right into the batter. Then there's the rava kichadi – a wheat-based semolina mixed with vegetables. The sambar is also recommended – a lentil-based vegetable stew, which originates from Tamil Nadu. Both Woodlands and Sangeetha can provide Jain food on request – vegetarian food that among other things, doesn't include root vegetables such as garlic and onion.

Jo Jo's Indian, Gaylord Indian and Joshan restaurants, which appear elsewhere in the food section, also provide great South Indian dishes and vegetarian food.

Here are the addresses for the vegetarian restaurants mentioned above.

_____

≡ **Woodlands International Restaurant**
  UG 16-17, Wing On Plaza, 62 Mody Rd, Tsim Sha Tsui.
  Tel: 2369 3718

≡ **Sangeetha Vegetarian Restaurant**
  UG 1-5 & 31, Wing On Plaza, 62 Mody Rd, Tsim Sha Tsui
  Tel: 2640 2123

≡ **Saravanaa Bhavan**
  4/F, Ashley Centre, 23-25 Ashley Road, Tsim Sha Tsui
  Tel: 2736 1127

≡ **Branto Pure Veg Indian Restaurant**
  1/F, 9 Lock Road, Tsim Sha Tsui
  Tel: 2366 8171

→ *Eating Your Way Round 'Little Nepal in Jordan'*

It's early, just before lunchtime at the Manakamana Nepali Restaurant & Bar in the Jordan section of southern Kowloon. This unassuming restaurant is the place to go for both Nepalese and a number of Indian dishes. Recommended by Trip Advisor, restaurant guides and other Hong Kong forums, it provides a range of dishes from regular samosas and momos, to lamb rogan josh.

Susma Rana is a regular visitor to this part of Jordan. The daughter of a retired Gurkha officer, she's trilingual, speaking Nepali, Cantonese and English. There are a number of Nepalese restaurants in Jordan, where there are also Nepalese beauty salons, jewellers and provision stores.

→ Dal bhat, a dish of beans, lentils and boiled rice.

→ A traditional dried meat Nepalese dish available at The Hello Kitchen.

The Manakamana Nepali Restaurant & Bar is named after a temple near Kathmandu. "There's a cable car to go up and it was the first cable car in Nepal," says Susma, whose father now lives in Kathmandu.

Susma makes some recommendations and we order some light items, such as dumplings better known as momo. "When it comes to food, I get together with my friends and we have a momo party. Everyone loves momo! So we make them together and make three types: chicken, pork and vegetable."

For the minced pork, she says, you can add in extra fat to keep it juicy, plus red onions, garlic and salt. "The same for the chicken as it can be a bit lean, so you add in more butter and cabbage and keep it nice and juicy." The vegetable ones are self-explanatory. "Vegetarian is just vegetables!" she says.

Main courses at Manakamana Nepali Restaurant & Bar can be the more Indian butter chicken, lamb rogan josh, plus plenty of vegetarian and vegan fare, including dal. Save some space for the delicious ice-cream dessert, kulfi.

Two other recommended restaurants in the area are the Hungry Eye Restaurant and the Ex-Gorkha Restaurant, both in the same Jordan neighbourhood. They're not the poshest surroundings, the décor is simple, but the staff is friendly, the food is tasty and the price is very reasonable. Sometimes there can be a little bit of a wait, but that's often because the restaurants insist on using original ingredients and making everything from scratch.

A couple of minutes' walk away in Shanghai Street is The Hello Kitchen. Friendly staff members explain the dishes which mostly come in around the HK$50 mark, including a plate of momos or the vegetable thukpa noodle soup, accompanied by a reviving cup of masala tea for just $10. This is a street side eatery with a couple of tables.

For posher surroundings there's also the Nepal Restaurant in Staunton Street. But don't miss the chance to eat in Jordan, dai pai dong style, a Hong Kong version of open air, street stall dining. Check out the alleyways for a chance to eat Nepalese streetfood snacks. You can't beat a paper plate of 10 succulent chicken or vegetable momos, where the warm juice pours out as you take your first bite. There's also the sel roti, a traditional ring-shaped sweet Nepalese bread, great for dipping in tea. The bread is traditionally prepared during the Nepalese festivals of Dashain and Tihar.

Susma also enjoys making her own pickles and recalls her childhood in Shek Kong in the New Territories area of Hong Kong. "We grew up using very simple spices like coriander, cumin and turmeric. Dad didn't like his food too spicy. Turmeric also acts as a very good anti-inflammatory. And if you have problems sleeping, you can boil up some milk and add in some honey for sweetness and add in some turmeric."

At the end of the meal, it's nice to wash it down with a masala tea – a tradition across the South Asian communities. And if you like it in the restaurant, says Susma, then you can always also make it at home.

"You need cinnamon, cloves and cardamom," she says. "Just bash it a bit slightly and just bruise it a bit. You can use loose tea or tea bags, and then maybe one cup of milk and half a cup of water depending on how rich and creamy you want it and you can add honey or sugar, depending on how sweet you want it. You can always buy it ready-made but it's easy to make your own."

Here are the addresses for the Nepalese restaurants mentioned above and some other choices.

──────────────

≡ **The Hello Kitchen**
185, Shanghai Street, Yau Ma Tei
Tel: 2626 0222

≡ **Manakamana Nepali Restaurant**
165 Temple Street, Jordan
Tel: 2385 2070

≡ **Ex-Gorkha Restaurant & Bar**
Shop 5, G/F, Kings Court,
67-75 Wai Ching Street, Jordan
Tel: 3954 5247

≡ **Hungry Eye Restaurant & Bar**
3/F, Gofuku Tower, 62-64 Woosung Street, Jordan
Tel: 3107 1115

≡ **Nepal Restaurant**
G/F., 14 Staunton Street, SoHo, Central
Tel: 2869 6212

≡ **Himalaya Restaurant**
1/F A, 20-30 Tai Wong Street East, Wan Chai
Tel: 2527 5899

→ *Sri Lankan Food – a Culinary Mission*

Sri Lankan foodies have a mission. They want you to know that Sri Lankan cuisine is something you will enjoy learning about. And by the way, it is distinct from its Indian counterpart.

Hongkongers are gradually getting a chance to learn about the diverse foods from this small nation shaped like a teardrop at the base of India. From the 16th century onwards at least parts of Sri Lanka were occupied by different European powers – these included the Portuguese, Dutch and finally the British. Sri Lankans combined the cooking techniques of all these nationalities, adopting their ideas or mixing them with their Sinhalese, Tamil and Muslim dishes, to form their own distinct cuisine.

→ The traditional egg hopper.

→ Devilled fish curry – fish with spices onion, peppers and chilli.

Lamprais, which we'll hear more about later, is actually "lump rice" – a dish created by the Dutch Burghers in Sri Lanka. Burghers are Eurasians of mixed Dutch, Portuguese and Sri Lankan descent.

Sri Lankan food centres around rice with curries. Its sauces are often sweet and spicy filled with cardamom, ginger, all homegrown, and cinnamon. Sri Lankan cinnamon can be more expensive, but the Sri Lankan owner of Hong Kong restaurant Serendib, claims is the best in the world.

There are two Sri Lankan restaurants in the city, one in Sheung Wan on Hong Kong island, the other in Saikung in the New Territories. Another restaurant on Lamma Island in Yung Shue Wan offers Sri Lankan fare on its menu. At Serendib on Wing Lok Street in Sheung

Wan, the cheerful owner is on a mission to introduce Sri Lankan food to the office workers who throng to his 30-seat restaurant. His name is Davenarayana Acharige Damesh Niroshan but he adds helpfully: "They call me Damesh or Niro." The word has got out about his reasonably priced Sri Lankan street food, which he cooks himself at his ground floor eatery just past the antique stores and wholesale shops selling sweets and nuts. Commuters flock to the place at lunch hour for meals starting at HK$60 with drinks.

Serendib is an old Persian name for Sri Lanka. Damesh comes from Negombo on the island's west coast. His wife, a Hong Kong Chinese named Veronica Wong, is co-owner of this popular eatery. They serve street food that you'd find walking down the streets of Sri Lanka's capital Colombo, or further south down the coast in Galle, or up in the lush tea plantations of central Nuwara Eliya.

"We keep a simple menu of Sri Lankan street food," says Damesh. "Many people in Hong Kong don't know what Sri Lankan food is, so we are introducing them to dishes like chicken kottu – where you use a flatbread, such as a roti, and then mix it with chicken and vegetables. That's very typical."

"How would I describe Sri Lankan food? Spicy and sweet," says Veronica, who has enjoyed bringing Sri Lankan food to her Hong Kong neighbours. There are a number of vegetarian options on the menu, including vegetable samosas. Damesh does all the cooking. Another Sri Lankan staple – the hopper – a bowl-shaped crepe that you can fill with an egg or curry or pickles, is a bit tricky to pull off when you're a one man band and have plenty of people waiting. So at Serendib they plan to have specific "hopper nights".

There's the dal vade – a tasty street food popular in both Sri Lanka and South India – a patty made of dal or split peas, mixed with onion, turmeric, curry, red chilli and ginger and then fried in oil. And the devilled fish – a fried fish tempered with sweet and sour sauce. This is popular as a side dish in Sri Lanka and also reflects the island nation's Portuguese and Dutch heritage.

→ Serendib owners Veronica Wong and Damesh Niroshan.

"For the devilled fish, it needs to be spicy and a little sweet," says Damesh. "I use a lot of cinnamon, cardamom, curry powder, cloves, ginger, and garlic." Damesh has been in Hong Kong for six years. Both he and Veronica have been together for 10 years; they married in 2011. They met on a Japanese course in Japan and communicate with one another in Japanese.

Serendib also serves a Sri Lankan dish with a Dutch heritage – lamprais – rice, meat and vegetables packed in coconut leaves. The leaves, Veronica takes from her aunt's garden in Hong Kong to wrap the rice. "It's wrapped in the leaf and baked in an oven."

"Hong Kong people tend to mix up Sri Lankan with Indian food," says Veronica. "So it is a bit of a challenge for us. They often are not sure where Sri Lanka is. But they are always willing to try new food! Some say it's too spicy, others think it is not spicy enough!"

Damesh sources his ingredients directly from Sri Lanka. "The Sri Lankan cinnamon is regarded as the best," he says. Some of his items come through Pearl Ocean Foods & Spices Organic Limited, an online delivery service in Hong Kong, based at Tuen Mun and To Kwa Wan. The Sri Lankan black tea is directly sourced from Sri Lanka where Damesh has contacts at the plantations.

Veronica also recommends their soursop – a wood apple juice, where the pulp is brought directly from Sri Lanka.

Here are the addresses for the Sri Lankan restaurants mentioned above and some other choices.

———————————

≡ Serendib
   Shop 2, GF, Nam Wo Hong Building, 148 Wing Lok street, Sheung Wan
   Tel: 3705 2429
   Lunch starting from $60 including drinks.

≡ AJ's Sri Lankan Cuisine
   G/F, 14 Sai Kung Hoi Pong Street, Sai Kung
   Tel: 2792 2555

≡ The Waterfront Restaurant & Bar
   (serves some Sri Lankan dishes)
   58 Yung Shue Wan Main Street, Lamma Island
   Tel: 2982 1168

North Indian Dishes

↑ *Navratan Korma*

A delicious North Indian dish that has nuts, paneer and cheese mixed with vegetables. Navratan means nine gems referring to the nine different types of vegetables, fruit and other ingredients. It is a rich curry that can be used as a side dish with roti or any flavoured rice. It's a "Mughlai" dish, so dating back to the Mughals and is wonderfully over the top with raisins, cashew nuts and cherries.

↑ *Shahi Paneer*

A North Indian curry made using cottage cheese in thick gravy made up of spices, tomatoes, onion and cream. Usually eaten with rice, roti or naan. The tomato gravy uses cashew nuts to give it a rich texture.

↑ Butter Chicken

Butter chicken is apparently called Butter Chicken because it has chunks of grilled chicken prepared in a makhani or butter gravy that uses butter and cream in its recipe along with tomato puree and spices such as masala, ginger, garlic, coriander and dry fenugreek powder. After being marinated for several hours the chicken can be cooked in a tandoor or traditional clay oven, or be grilled, roasted or pan fried.

↑ Samosas

Along with the banana, the samosa must count as one of the world's most compact, instant and easy to eat – plus delicious street foods. The samosa is triangular in shape, with fried pastry on the outside and on the inside spiced potatoes and peas with broken cashews. It is traditionally served with yoghurt and mint chutney.

← Aloo Gobi

A tasty dish that can be found in North India but is also eaten in Bangladesh, Pakistan and Nepal. It's a vegetarian mix of potatoes, cauliflower and Indian spices.

South Indian Dishes

↑ *Iddli*

↑ *Medu Vada*

What chappatis are to North India, iddlis are to the South – albeit with much more preparation. The chappatis can be made in a couple of minutes, whereas the iddlis take a bit longer. A batter made of dehusked fermented black lentils is steamed and then served hot with condiments such as sambar or chutney for this South Indian breakfast staple.

Another South Indian breakfast favourite is the medu vada, an Indian fritter made from mungo bean. It's formed into a doughnut shape with a crispy outside and soft inside. It's a popular South Indian daily snack that is also a key component of the menu on festival days. It can be served as a main course, side dish or snack. They are served with sambar and coconut chutney.

↑ Uthamppam

This is a pancake made with iddli batter and vegetables. You can put whatever you like in them, a mix of vegetables or other ingredients. The vegetables are cut into the batter and then cooked.

↑ Rasam

Rasam is another South Indian staple. A good comfort food filled with garlic and spices. There's any number of rasam varieties, including tomato. It's seen as a comfort food but also as a way to get rid of a cold due to the garlic, turmeric and other ingredients. Rasam originated in Tamil Nadu and Karnataka.

← Dosa

The dosa is a type of pancake that looks like a crepe. It's made with fermented batter made out of rice and black lentils. The fillings vary, but a yummy way to start the day is a breakfast of dosa stuffed with potato, fried onion and spices.

Traditional Nepalese Dishes

↑ *Gundruk*

This is widely regarded as a Nepalese national staple made from dried mustard, cauliflower and radish leaves. When the vegetables are harvested in the autumn, the leftover leaves are dried and fermented along with the radish roots to make an appetizer or side dish to accompany the main meal. Some Nepalese restaurants also take the fermented, pickled vegetables and turn them into Gundruk soup.

↑ *Momo*

A delicious and simple dumpling that can contain chicken, vegetables or pork. The ingredients are wrapped in the dough and then steamed. The momos are often eaten with a tomato sauce.

↑ *Thukpa*

Thukpa is a Tibetan noodle soup that can be vegetarian or made with chicken. A hearty winter meal, it's sort of a cross between a noodle soup and ramen. The dish is a tasty combination of vegetables, chicken for protein, and noodles, sometimes made from buckwheat.

↑ *Sel Roti*

Sel roti are a traditional Nepalese bread made in the shape of a ring. They're sweet and can be found in the Nepalese heart of Jordan along Battery Street and Temple Street. Great to eat as a snack by themselves, they also work well dipped in tea. The main ingredients are rice flour, water, sugar, butter, cardamom and cloves.

← *Dal Bhat*

Dal bhat is a dish eaten across the Indian sub-continent, and is very popular throughout Nepal. The main ingredients are beans or lentils and boiled rice. But in Nepal as you go to higher elevations in the Himalayas, where rice no longer grows, boiled rice is replaced by millet, buckwheat or barley. Dal bhat is made using lentils or beans cooked with garlic, onion, tomatoes, tamarind, ginger and chili and can include spices and herbs such as coriander, turmeric, garam masala and cumin.

Sri Lankan Dishes

↑ *Hoppers*

Hoppers are bowl-shaped Sri Lankan pancake or crepe. Made from rice flour and fermented coconut milk, they are fried in a bowl-shaped pan, smaller than a wok. They can be eaten just as they are with a bit of salt and pepper or be served with an egg and some form of curry or relish. Lunumiris, a spicy paste that is presented as a condiment, is often served with hoppers.

↑ *Lamprais*

Lamprais is a rice dish with Dutch influences. Sri Lanka's diverse food reflects the many nations that have influenced its history. It's a rice dish packaged in a banana leaf and the name is derived from the Dutch "lomprijst", generally meaning "a packet of food".

↑ *Kottu Roti*

A highly popular street food, this mishmash of items works well any time – late at night or for breakfast. Roti – also known as chapati, the South Asian flatbread – is chopped up into small pieces and then mixed with eggs and vegetables, including cabbage, onions and leek. It can also include chicken, beef, or mutton.

↑ *Watalappan*

Watalappan is particularly popular among Sri Lankan Muslims. It's the "crème caramel" equivalent of this teardrop nation. The steamed caramel custard has cane sugar, nutmeg, crushed cardamom pod seeds, vanilla and chopped cashew nuts among its ingredients. It's one of the most beloved desserts and is served at parties and weddings.

← *Devilled Fish Curry*

Add "devilled" to anything and it means mixing in lots of spices, and in this particular dish, you also have the infusion of Dutch and Portuguese culinary influences. This curry can be made with any "firm" fish that won't flake. Marinate the fish with onion, peppers, chilli, crushed red pepper and salt.

Bangladeshi Dishes

Bangladeshi food is available in Indian and Pakistani restaurants in Hong Kong. The food is halal. Bangladesh is the world's largest delta, formed by three great rivers, so fish – alongside rice and dairy products – is a big part of the diet.

Here are five typical Bangladeshi dishes:

Beef Kala Bhuna

This is a favourite meal for Bangladeshis, and originates in the southeastern city of Chittagong. Red meat is added to a thick, rich sauce filled with spices, including ground ginger, and using lots of ghee. In this case, it's with beef, but can also make use of chicken or vegetables, served up with white or flatbreads such as luchi, or paratha.

Chingri Malai Curry

This is a prawn curry made from prawns and coconut milk. The curry is flavoured with turmeric powder, green chili, garlic, ginger and mustard oil, along with onions. Garam masala is sprinkled on the top before the curry is served with rice.

Luchi

This is a Bengali speciality. Puffed bread, which is made from flour and stays white in colour and is fried in oil. Not the healthiest item, but yum!

Sorshe Ilish

This is a popular dish both in Bangladesh and West Bengal in India. The main ingredient is the ilish, a type of herring and Bangladesh's national fish. The fish is cooked and then mixed with a sautéed mustard sauce.

Malai Chomchom Sweets

This very popular dessert is tough on the outside, soft on the inside with milk and vinegar used to create the chhena, a cheese curd that is made from water buffalo or cow's milk. Pistachios and saffron, as well as sugar and green cardamom are added for this very sweet treat.

Pakistani Dishes

Lucknowi Nihari

This is a slow-cooked stew with lamb shank, left to marinate for a day before being cooked for at least three hours. It's a traditional dish of Muslims of New Delhi, Bhopal and Lucknow.

Karachi Kadai Chicken

Kadai chicken is a dish cooked by both Pakistanis and North Indians. The kadai or kahari is a bowl-shaped frying pan with two handles. The chicken is cooked for 30-50 minutes with cumin, tomatoes and ginger. The Punjabi version also uses bell peppers and onions.

Peshawari Chappali Kebab

Minced lamb kebabs made from herbs, spices, eggs, pomegranate seeds and ginger. Served with an apricot-jaggery-raisin sauce. It is usually made from minced ground beef or mutton and various spices, shaped into a patty. It originates from Peshawar in northwest Pakistan.

Hyderabadi Mutton Biryani

This is a speciality of Hyderabad in Sindh province. The mutton is marinated and then layered with half-cooked rice in a pot and then cooked together.

Hari Mirch Ka Keema

Minced lamb and green peas cooked with onion and garlic and finished with fresh coriander.

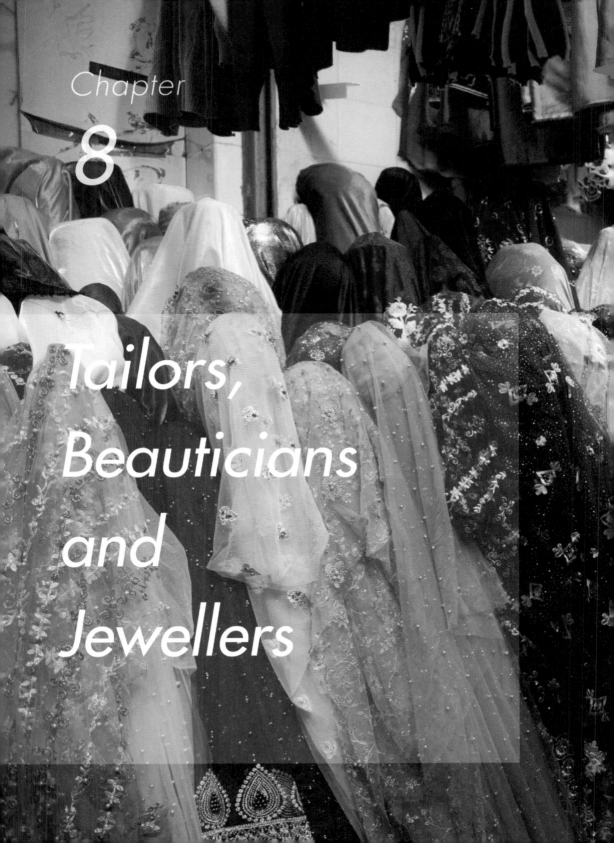

Chapter

8

Tailors,
Beauticians
and
Jewellers

Tailors, Beauticians and Jewellers

→ *Sam's Tailor*

There's a good feeling about wearing something that has been made just for you. The cut of the cloth fits neatly around the neck and wrists and it's fun to be able to choose colours, patterns and types of material. Hong Kong is a place known for making suits in 24 hours. Its tailors, many of them Indian, have been in the business for decades. Some establishments date back to the late 19th century and a number made their business serving British officers and soldiers. Shirts and blouses are available at HK$400 up, and a good suit will be set you back by about HK$4,000. Bear in mind that some but not all tailors are also dressmakers. Sanskrit at the more exclusive end of the price spectrum, listed below, also provides bespoke clothing made by Indian designers as well as Indian jewellery and accessories, including beaded bags. Shop around, as prices vary, with five

→ Manu Melwani, owner of Sam's Tailor, measures customer Bill Stewart in his shop in Tsim Sha Tsui.

recommendations below and where to find them in Hong Kong and Kowloon. Among them is the famed Sam's Tailor.

Sam's Tailor in Tsim Sha Tsui is synonymous with high quality bespoke tailoring and some rather famous clients. Britain's Queen Elizabeth II, actress Sigourney Weaver, past American presidents, singer and actress Kylie Minogue – and the list goes on.

TV journalists also flock to Sam's Tailor in Nathan Road's Burlington Arcade for that special setting that says this is Hong Kong. But it wasn't always like this for this successful Indian family.

Chapter 8 —— Tailors, Beauticians and Jewellers

That becomes clear when Manu Melwani, who helped his father, Naraindas Melwani, set up the business in Hong Kong in the late 1950s, starts to recount the story of his childhood.

"We came to Hong Kong in October 1957. I was born in 1948 and from a young age my brother, sister and I were helping my father to build up his business, especially with British soldiers and officers here. We built it up slowly.

"We came over on an Air India flight in October 1957. My father didn't know how to do business. I didn't know how to speak Chinese, and slowly we started."Mr Melwani attended St George's School, which had been set up in 1955 to serve the educational needs of the children of armed forces personnel and civil servants. "There was a discount, so it was cheap education," he says. "My first language was Sindhi, which my mother spoke to me. Tailoring was the only business of which my father had any knowledge. He didn't know about jewellery or diamonds, it was very hard for him to learn something. A lot of Sindhis are mostly exporters – they mostly export their goods from Hong Kong to the Middle East and America – they were middle people."

While Mr Melwani was supporting his father from a young age, in 1975 he had the chance to go for professional training at the prestigious Saville Row in London. "These English guys taught me everything about the business," he says. But it wasn't easy. He worked for free as an apprentice and only received his food as payment. He and the other apprentices slept in the workshop. His training was cut short when his mother became ill in Hong Kong and he had to return, but what he learned, he feels, sets him apart from other tailors.

His son, Roshan Melwani, is the third generation of Melwanis to run Sam's Tailor. But that wasn't automatic. Roshan went to New York University, he worked for professional services business Herbert Smith Freehills and then created two start-up businesses in the UK - one was a personal concierge service, the other was an online auction site. But then he decided to give the family business a try, and has

→ Manu Melwani at the entrance of the legendary Sam's Tailor in Tsim Sha Tsui.

been instrumental in taking the firm forward.

"I warned him that it's very tough – you get a lot of abuse from the customers, if the suit is not right," says Manu Melwani. "You have to be very patient and understand what the client wants."

In the shop space, the Melwanis work with their Chinese tailor, who is 70. "We call him sugar daddy," jokes Manu. "I know his father because his father worked with us too. He's very patient with me. This guy has been working with me for 35 years." But there are around 60 tailors working for Sam's Tailor in total.

Manu Melwani's stellar reputation has been built on his quality workmanship but also his level of discretion. He has worked with

→ (Top and Bottom) Shop assistant Dalbir Kaur
helps a customer choose fabrics at Samina
Fashion House.

various members of the British royal family, including Queen
Elizabeth II, but you won't hear from him what she requested. As
well as men's clothing, Sam's Tailor also can make cocktail dresses,
ball gowns and other clothing for women clients.

Hong Kong is famous for the 24-hour suit. But for Mr Melwani,
that's just coasting. He says the fastest handiwork – for him and
eight of his workers – was two hours and 30 minutes, when he
was raising funds for the Christmas charity fundraising campaign
Operation Santa Claus, jointly organized by Radio Television Hong
Kong (RTHK) and the *South China Morning Post* newspaper. The
suit was cut and sewn at the Hilton Hotel in the late 1980s, and for
a while it was a Guinness World Record, says Mr Melwani.

Roshan Melwani grew up with the business, working his holidays in
the shop. "I'm living proof of child labour in China. They put me
to work Easter, Christmas and summer holidays from age 11 to 16.
But there was always something amazing here. I'd come and see my
grandfather and look up at all the photos of all these famous people.
And I now see my kids doing that as well."

Roshan Melwani joined the business 19 years ago. "It was a great
business, it was a very different business at the time, to what we are

now. It was a very successful business. It sounds harsh to say but it was perhaps on the brink of being relegated to the dark ages. And luckily, we have evolved over the past 19 years to what we are now. I started to rebuild the business. And now I like to go to sleep so I can get up and come here the following day."

The Melwanis now have 14 premises in the same building that they have procured over time. But they have been careful to stay true to their origins.

"All our workers work for us, they don't moonlight," he says. "They are there for us, we are their direct employer. Obviously the quality is paramount. Without that level of quality, then there is no success. We work and we live in a very competitive industry. We choose to be a small fish, we choose to work in a niche environment. So we have just under 60 tailors working for us, and then 15 consultants. So it is a large team. And we are purely retail. We don't go on the road. We don't have a factory churning stuff out, we don't outsource. We just make clothes for our retail clients and we see up to 30 people a day.

"That makes us truly unique."

Roshan Melwani likes to work with leading fabric brands "because I believe in transparency. You're coming to me for the tailoring and you're coming to me for me. The fabric should be independent. I want to use leading brands because they've done the R&D, they've done the testing. It's top of the line, available all over the world, from companies with massive levels of accountability."

As well as taking Sam's Tailor forward, Roshan Melwani is a firm believer in leading from the front in terms of his commitment to the community. "I'm very heavily involved in the Kowloon Cricket Club and I support the cricket section in any which way I can," he says. "I'm also involved in a Sindhi organization that's been around since 1964. I was formerly its president. It's called The Young Executives Group. I have organized Diwali balls, a plethora of them, I've MCed, I've danced on stage. I've done everything I can do to move my community forward in a wholesome manner. I believe wholeheartedly in community.

"I know without a doubt I'm uber successful because of a platform has been provided to me by Indians, by Sindhis, who have trailblazed before. So I've had this wonderful platform that has been carved out by both my father's hard work and the rest of the Indians in his generation."

Here are the addresses for the tailor shop mentioned above and some other choices.

≡ **Sam's Tailor**
90-94C Nathan Road
Burlington Arcade, Tsim Sha Tsui
Tel: 2367 9423

≡ **Raja Fashions**
Bespoke Tailors
34-C Cameron Road, G/F.,Tsim Sha Tsui, Kowloon
Tel: 2366 7624

≡ **Sanskrit**
Bespoke designers, bridal wear, occasion wear, kaftans, tunics, elaborate saris. Viewings by appointment only.
Suite 1604, 1 Lyndhurst Terrace,
Central, Hong Kong
Tel: 2545 2088

≡ **Star Tailors**
Room 734, 7/F, Star House,
No. 3 Salisbury Road, Tsim Sha Tsui
Mobile: 9127 5206

≡ **Apsley (Established 1889)**
Bespoke Tailors
Shop G & H, G/F Burlington House, 90-94c Nathan Road, Tsim Sha Tsui,
Tel: 2366 6612

→ Beauty Salons

Across Hong Kong, there are a number of Indian and Nepalese beauty salons, some providing a luxurious pampering, others a fast and no frills way to get ready ahead of a night out, or to really go all out ahead of a party, wedding or other special occasion. These include hair waxing, eyebrow and face threading, or simply coming in to the salon for a wash, cut and blow dry. If you want the whole deal – try a relaxing, rejuvenating facial followed by a skilled make-up artist making you party ready. And, hey, have a shoulder massage, while you're there. Go spoil yourself, with prices, particularly in Kowloon, that are very affordable.

Prices range from just HK$25 up for eyebrow or upper lip threading, to facials beginning at HK$250 and climbing to HK$600 or more -

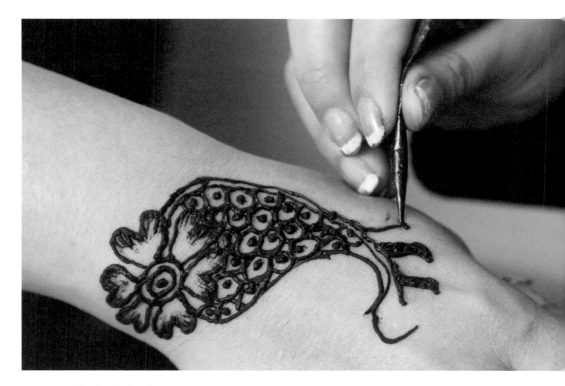

→ An example of mehndi or henna art.

252

→ Nepalese beautician Jharana Bhujel applies henna art on a client's hand and arm.

depending on the treatment and location of the salon. Party make-up comes in at around HK$200-$400 and there's also bridal make-up for that very special occasion. For the full wedding preparation, there's also mehndi, the ancient practice of henna decoration for hands and other parts of the body.

So let's take a look at some of these South Asian beauty techniques. Mehndi, the ancient technique of applying henna art on the body, can be traced back to India, but is also popular these days in Nepal and other countries in the Middle East and around the Mediterranean. The henna is first mixed with water and made into a paste in a cone. The end of the cone is then snipped off and the henna applied in the same way that you might pipe decorations on to a cake.

Chapter 8 —— Tailors, Beauticians and Jewellers

→ (Top) Examples of evening hairstyles on offer at Image Hair Salon in Jordan.

→ (Bottom) A beautician, Jyoti Gurung at Image Hair Salon in Jordan works on a client's hair.

Nepalese beautician Jharana Bhujel is an expert. At Super Angelic Hair and Beauty Salon on Shanghai Street in Jordan, she is deft and fast, as she applies the henna. Her prices start at HK$50 depending on how involved the henna art is.

Nowadays, henna art is very popular at weddings in Nepal as well, a fashion that has caught on from India in the past one to two generations. In Rajasthan, in northern India, the groom is likely to have as much intricate henna decoration drawn on his body as his bride.

Often ahead of a wedding, female relatives and friends of the bride will also have some henna decoration drawn on the palms of their hand, while for the bride it will be the front and back of the hands, plus her arms going up to the elbows. Designs include flowers, hearts, birds including peacocks, and can also be anything that the client requests. The henna decoration gradually fades with immersion in water – a good excuse to get someone else to do the dishes for a few days!

To help the colour to stay, you can also apply a mix of lemon and sugar and dab it on with cotton wool. If you want to have a go yourself, the henna is available at Indian and Nepalese stores in Hong Kong, but at the reasonable prices here, it might be better left to the professionals!

Sunita Gurung, who comes from Baudha near Kathmandu, has been working at Image Hair Salon on Battery Street in the Jordan area for nearly three years. It's one of three salons owned by manager Indra Gurung.

Threading is an art of hair removal that involves a cotton thread which is held in the hands of the beautician. With one part of the string in her mouth, she efficiently works away on removing hair to shape the eyebrow.

Sunita explains how she threads a client's eyebrows: "I use a cotton thread like a string," she says. "You have to put powder on the eyebrow first. Then you hold down one part of the string before wrapping it around your fingers three times. You do the same with your other hand, so you create a 'triangle of string'" to pluck or thread the hairs row by row. Threading for eyebrows can be as little as HK$20.

At Khoob Surat in Mirador Mansions in Tsim Sha Tsui, Harpreet Kaur and her colleagues specialize in massages, facials and waxing. For waxing there are treatments using tea tree wax, fruit wax or sugar, ranging from half leg at HK$60 to full body at HK$460. A rejuvenating 20-minute head and shoulder massage is a bargain at HK$60 and there are around 15 types of facials to choose from. There's also a happy hour special rate from Monday to Saturday from 2:00 pm to 4:00 pm where customers are treated to a discount on eyebrow threading.

Some salons also provide manicures and pedicures.

Back at Image Hair Salon, the beauticians cover all the bases – apart from pedicures and manicures. So they cut and colour hair, thread eyebrows, apply stunningly artistic mehndi, and even provide tattoos, from simple artwork to bigger designs as well as eyebrow tattooing and piercing. There's also waxing and make-up available. A steady stream of largely Nepalese male and female clients file through the shop all afternoon. Due to its competitive prices, Image Hair Salon is also a go-to destination for domestic helpers for beauty treatments on their days off.

Anita Gurung is busy colouring a client's hair after showing some samples. The client is a European looking to cover a bit of grey. "It's better to go a darker brown," advises Anita, "red shades will not cover the grey strands." Anita arrived in Hong Kong at the age of 16, 20 years ago. The salon is nestled in what Anita describes as "Little Nepal" around Battery Street in Jordan.

Nepalese beauty salons are available for a variety of services throughout Hong Kong and particularly in Nepalese communities such as Jordan and Yuen Long, where prices will be cheaper than on Hong Kong Island. While we talk, two young Nepalese men wander in and ask for nose piercings. Their skin is cleaned, their noses pierced, studs inserted. Two contented young men check the results in the mirror and happily saunter out – all in less than 15 minutes.

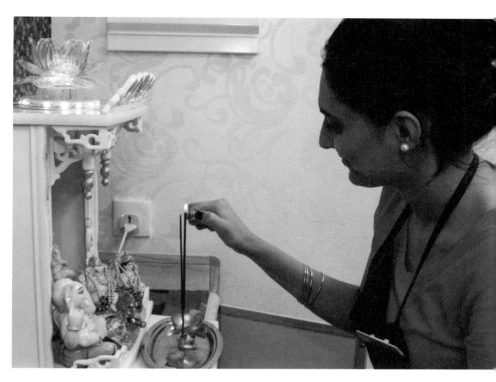

→ An employee of Freedas Salon lights incense at a small shrine.

Riviea Beauty Salon in Central gets good reviews. Expect to pay more, the business is in a high rent district, but provides a professional and friendly atmosphere and a chance to feel pampered with a relaxing facial.

Riviea also provides online advice on how you can look after your face, particularly with Hong Kong's air pollution at times, while you're away from the salon. Here's one treatment:

For normal skin care, you can take one cup of yoghurt, one tablespoon of orange juice and one tablespoon of lemon juice and mix it into a paste. Apply it on your face as a mask and keep it on for 15 minutes. Then clean it off with a wet tissue and watch your complexion glow! For dry skin, you could use a mixture of cooked oatmeal and honey; it will not only help moisturize the skin but also acts as a good cleansing agent.

For another relaxing experience at an Indian salon, Freedas Salon has two outlets, one situated on Caine Road and the other in Tsim Sha Tsui. Freedas also provides manicures and pedicures as well as waxing and threading.

The abundance of Indian and Nepalese salons means you can have a professional see to your needs while you lie back and take the weight off your feet. If you fancy products for do-it-yourself treatment at home, Himalaya Herbals have a selection of face scrubs, lotions and moisturizers that you can find at some of the Indian or Nepalese provision stores in the Jordan area. Meanwhile, sit back and relax and allow these longstanding salons to leave you refreshed and rejuvenated.

Here are the addresses for the beauty salons mentioned above and some other choices.

≡ **Image Hair Salon**
46 Battery Street, Jordan
2374 0455

≡ **Riviea Beauty Salon**
4/F Winner Building, 37 D'Aguilar Street, Central Hong Kong
Tel: 2892 0839

≡ **Freedas Salon**
86-88 Nathan Road, Comfort Building, Tsim Sha Tsui
Tel: 3580 0447

≡ **Khoob Surat – A Ladies Beauty Parlour**
1/F, Shop No. 25, Mirador Mansion, Tsim Sha Tsui, Kowloon
Tel: 2367 7742

≡ **Freedas**
Mezz Floor, 124 Caine Road, Hong Kong
Tel: 3580 0405

→ Kulbir Singh Dhaliwal checks for the delivery time of the Alphonso mangoes outside New Delhi Store on the ground floor of Chungking Mansions in Tsim Sha Tsui.

→ *South Asian Merchandise Stores*

Hong Kong has a good collection of stores carrying South Asian provisions. They can be found on Hong Kong Island, in Kowloon's Tsim Sha Tsui and Jordan areas and Yuen Long in the New Territories, among other areas. They carry an array of spices, pulses, and rice, as well as clothing, accessories and devotional items. Bags of turmeric are available for as little as HK$10. You can gather the ingredients to make your own masala tea, or cheat with the instant packs. There are sticks of cinnamon, cloves, and Himalayan rock salt. Just breathe it in and you can feel yourself being transported to Rajasthan or the Sri Lankan coast. Part of the fun is heading into the stores and searching for fresh products to do your own cooking. But if you prefer home delivery, there are also online options to choose from.

Chapter 8 —— Tailors, Beauticians and Jewellers

Here is a thumbnail sketch of two shops in Tsim Sha Tsui and in Jordan with a brief introduction from their proprietors. (Other similar stores can be found throughout Hong Kong).

Kulbir Singh Dhaliwal, 51, came to Hong Kong from Punjab in India in 1990. He is the manager of the New Delhi Store on the ground floor of the venerable Chungking Mansions in Tsim Sha Tsui.

"Our shop opened in 1974," he says, adding it was originally run by his father-in-law, Karam Singh Khosa, and Mr Khosa's brother-in-law, Mukhtiar Singh Brar.

"We were in Kimberley Street before, and then we moved to Chungking Mansions around 1977. My father-in-law came to Hong Kong in 1957. Both of them worked as doormen at the Mandarin Hotel" – now the Mandarin Oriental.

After his father-in-law died in 1990, Mr Singh took over the business with Mukhtiar Singh Brar's son and they have been running it ever since.

The shop has a wide selection of ready-made curry sauces, or you can make up your own with the variety of spices on display. There's turmeric, cumin, lotus root, to name a few.

"We import wheat flour from Canada, rice from Pakistan, and pulses, spices, and pickles from India," he says. "We also import Scotch whisky and single malts as well as Indian whiskies. There's also McDowell's No.1 [Reserve Whisky], which has an awesome taste. We also have good quality spices for curries, biryanis, everything."

For breakfast, Mr Singh, a father of three, eats just simple bread, he says. "We call it paratha or chapati. Lunch and dinner are curry and rice with chapati."

Pakistani businessman and shopkeeper Ahmad, who runs Buraq Islamic Store, has had a shop on the ground floor of Chungking

→ (Top) The Siddha Baba General Store at New Reclamation Street in Jordan.

→ (Bottom) Pakistani businessman and shopkeeper Ahmad at his Buraq Islamic Store in Chungking Mansions.

→ Shopowner Arif Khan owns the Jalalia Provision Store in Kwai Chung.

Mansions in Tsim Sha Tsui for nearly 20 years, and has lived in the city for 30 years. Originally from Lahore, Ahmad, who prefers to go by just his first name, went into business selling mobile accessories but then switched to Islamic products for Muslim clients from the South Asian communities, the Middle East, Africa and Indonesia.

"I have dates from Iran, Tunisia, Algeria and Saudi Arabia," he says, pointing to boxes stacked at the front of the shop. "Dates are important, because they are good for health." During Ramadan they are often used as the item of food to break the fast at dusk.

Ahmad also sells electronic Quran pens which automatically recite a verse from the Muslim holy book when passed over designated portions of the text.

→ An abundance of Saris and fabrics to choose at the Indian fashion House in Kwai Chung.

Sela, a Muslim from Indonesia who works as a domestic helper, is one of his regular customers. "I bought these pens for my friends," she says, "as often they don't speak Arabic, this helps them practise reciting the Quran."

There's honey from Egypt and Pakistan, miswak chewing sticks from the arak tree for cleaning teeth, hair dye, items of clothing for both Muslim men and women, as well as prayer mats from Saudi Arabia, Pakistan and Turkey.

There are simple, zip-up purses with a little compass embedded in the side, so that Muslims who carry them always know which way to face Mecca when it is time to pray.

Chapter 8 —— Tailors, Beauticians and Jewellers

There are digital clocks set for the five prayer calls throughout the day, and framed decorative verses of the Quran.

"I buy everything for prayer here," says Sela. "For our prophet Muhammad, beads, clothes, and halal make up. The perfume is halal as it has no alcohol. I've been in Hong Kong for eight years and sometimes go to the mosque in Tsim Sha Tsui and sometimes to the ones in Chai Wan and Wan Chai."

Heading on up Nathan Road from Tsim Sha Tsui you arrive in Jordan where Temple Street and the surrounding roads are home to a Nepalese community of provision stores, restaurants, beauty salons and jewellers.

At the Pashupati Store on Temple Street, there are bags of chura, rice that has been flattened into light, dry flakes. You can mix it with tea, milk and sugar. The chura soaks up the tea and it can be eaten as a snack. Further along the shelves are canned rasgulla, a syrupy dumpling made for those who love super-sweet Indian desserts. On the top shelf are pressure cookers. Nepalese enjoy the speed and convenience of pressure cookers, which save on time and energy. A breakfast of hot sweet potato can be ready in a flash and kept hot in a pressure cooker.

Move along the shelves, and there's mustard oil and black mustard seeds to make your own pickles, or buy the pickles and chutneys ready-made. Black and white Himalayan salt chunks, full of good minerals.

Cumin, coriander, turmeric, ginger, garlic paste are all there to make a basic but so tasty curry gravy.

On the other side of the shop are sarongs, or lungi, wrap-around skirts, as well as lightweight shirts and scarves.

Rice yeast is also for sale, for making rice or barley wine. The rice or barley is cooked and allowed to cool. Then you crush the rice yeast into a powder, sprinkle it over the rice, mix it, let it cool and bottle it up.

There's soap and henna hair dye. Pashupati is just one of several stores in this area.

Here are the addresses for the provision stores
mentioned above and some other choices.

≡ **New Delhi Store (Indian)**
22 & 26 Chungking Mansion, G/F
36-44 Nathan Road, Kowloon
Tel: 2369 3038 / 2369 0571

≡ **Pearl Ocean Food and Spices Organic Ltd (Sri Lankan)**
(Delivers a wide range of Sri Lankan provisions across Hong Kong)
Tel: 2790-2911

≡ **Maharaja Mart** (http://maharajamart.com/)
≡ **Star Mart Indian Grocery Store** (http://starmarthk.com/)
deliver to your door. (Indian)

≡ **Indian Provision Stores**
34 Bowrington Rd, Causeway Bay
Phone: 2891 8324

≡ **Ali Baba Provision Store (Pakistan, Bangladesh, Halal)**
20 Wood Rd, Morrison Hill, Wan Chai
Phone: 25749059

≡ **Pashupati Store (Nepalese)**
190 Temple Street, Yaumatei
Tel: 2770 5554

≡ **Buraq Islamic Store**
36C, G/F, Chungking Mansions,
36-44 Nathan Road, Tsim Sha Tsui, Kowloon

≡ **Lapha & Ngolsyo (Nepalese)**
All in One Store
147 Temple Street, Jordan, Kowloon
Tel: 2778 2499

→ Where to go for Nepalese jewellery

For Nepalese gold jewellery in Hong Kong, Kowloon is the place to go. One of the more popular places is Sanskriti Jewellers on Temple Street in Yau Ma Tei. They have been around for more than 10 years, and along with Indra Baraha Jewellery on Shanghai Street, in the neighbouring Jordan district, offer a wide selection of predominantly gold jewellery, including some magnificent wedding and ceremonial necklaces as well as chandelier earrings.

If you manage to attend one of the Nepalese festivals during the year, often in Hong Kong's country parks you'll likely see the kantha necklace, worn by girls and women of the Magar, Gurung, Kirat Rai and Limbu groups. It's quite large and comprises barrel shaped gold

→ Limu Sushmita wears a traditional outfit and jewellery including a bulaki through her nose at a festival celebrating Buddha Purnima at Kam Shan Country Park.

→ A staff member at Indra Baraha Jewellery shows an ornate silver filigree cover for a traditional Nepalese kukri knife.

beads interspersed with red felt pads. The necklace is a big statement piece that has a striking effect when worn along with traditional outfits.

Then there's the jun, which is gold, traditionally hand crafted and worn as an ornament on the head.

Like both Indians and Chinese, the Nepalese are fond of gold – both for gifts and as an easily transportable form of savings. The large display window at Sanskriti is a mass of yellow gold with large coin necklaces, that, interestingly, carry the image of the UK's Queen Elizabeth. Coin necklaces are particularly favoured by women in western Nepal, though often in silver rather than gold. These too indicate status and wealth.

Chapter 8 —— Tailors, Beauticians and Jewellers

→ (Top) A staff member shows a Nepalese gold bangle and gold coin ring at Indra Bahara Jewellery.

→ (Bottom) Nepalese young woman of the Gurung caste wear Kantha necklaces and traditional head ornaments.

The bulaki and the phuli are gold ornaments worn through the nose, particularly by Hindu Nepalese women. Other traditional Nepalese jewellery items include the suduk, which is particularly worn by Buddhist or Sherpa women. Made of gold or silver, and decorated with a precious stone of some sort, the suduk has a compartment inside where a religious mantra or sacred text can be placed to bring good fortune to the woman who wears it and protect her from bad luck.

Turquoise and coral necklaces are also popular, especially among Tibetans in Nepal. They will also mix in dzi beads of agate and gold. One of the most popular necklaces in Nepal is a strand of glass beads – usually worn as a symbol of marriage. These are called pote or tilhari if a gold pendant is added. Usually red beads are also part of the necklace and are worn only by married women.

Here are the addresses for the Nepalese jewellery stores mentioned above.

≡ **Sanskriti Jewellers Ltd**
   156 Temple Street, Yau Ma Tei, Kowloon
   Tel: 2771 8114

≡ **Indra Baraha Jewellery HK Ltd**
   191 Shanghai Street, Jordan, Kowloon

Chapter 8 —— Tailors, Beauticians and Jewellers

Classic, Earth and Chakra

Mala Daswani

→ Mala Daswani with bracelets and cuffs from the Chakra Jewellery Collection.

Mala Daswani turns the pages of an album that shows painted illustrations of her jewellery. The founder and creative force behind M&R Jewellers Ltd on Queen's Road in Central has formally been trained and is an expert on gemstones, but thrives on stripping the design right back to its origins and creating something unique and beautiful with her clients.

She's also an advocate of traditional Indian craftsmanship, championing complicated enamel work and firing, skills that are fast disappearing as people want immediate gratification. She has three collections of jewellery on show – some are ostentatious diamonds and gem stones, others in her Earth and Chakra collections show different facets of this designer who has lived in Hong Kong since the age of four.

"It feels like home, I've been here that long. If you gave me a choice between Indian and Chinese food, I'd probably go for Chinese," she says. Mala's training was in fashion and interior design and she started out employed by her father in his sari business, India Emporium, which was based in Hong Kong for many years, before her father departed for Dubai.

"My father is 80 odd years old now, he still goes to work every day," she says. Her parents had to leave Hyderabad, Sindh, what is Pakistan now, with "literally nothing" after British India was divided into two separate states in 1947. Then they settled in central India before coming later to Hong Kong. "Dad has been here since he was 20, working to build back."

Mala worked in her father's sari business for 18 months before taking a job at a jewellery firm in the city and then deciding to go for formal training.

"I got my degree at the Gemological Institute of America," says Mala describing the final exam. "There are 20 unknown stones and some of them could be glass. And you need to identify all 20 correctly. There is no margin for error." You get three chances, she says, not that she needed them, as she got all 20 first time round.

With support from her family and a lot of hard work, Mala built up her own business.

"So, you're invited to come and look at rough diamonds. It's called a site holding. Pretty much what you're offered, you take. And if you don't, generally you're not invited back. The larger diamonds could go to New York and Antwerp, the medium range, say to Israel, the smaller to India and to China. Although that is changing now."

Mala Daswani has three collections. "The primary is the classic diamond jewellery and the reason we got into this, is because when Indians get married, it's really an elaborate three, four, five days of festivities. It's something to celebrate when two families come together, it's never just about two people. The bride is always like a princess. They'll have three or four sets of jewellery, depending on the day."

"You'd have a diamond set, maybe a ruby one, maybe an emerald one. Also because of our background, jewellery is something we value, because it's easy to take in case you ever have to leave quickly. It's part of our background since the partition. So women were given jewellery, a gift from their parents."

Mala takes out a necklace made with uncut diamonds. "This is how they used to cut diamonds in the old days because they didn't have laboratories and electricity.

"These days you would have a wheel with diamond dust on it because the only thing that can cut a diamond is another diamond; it's the hardest thing on the planet. So you take the diamond on to the lap [the wheel] and cut 58 facets. You couldn't do that in the old days."

So prior to electricity, there could be about 16 facets on a diamond. "So on pieces like that they still use the same technique to get the old cut, they are called mine cuts, rose cuts, old cuts in different parts of the world."

Older Indian craftsmanship is showcased in a fabulous set of a choker, earrings and bracelet. "This piece is over 50 years old," she says, taking the choker out of the cabinet. "There is enamel working in Europe, too, like the Faberge eggs, but it's a different style. This piece has 16-facet diamonds."

She says only master craftsman can now make these kinds of pieces. And the way in which the enamel is heated at the end is really a master's skill. "If you don't heat it well it will crack. It's one of the final stages because you have to mould it and shape it – you would have to start all over again."

In addition to the diamond range of what one might expect for Indian wedding jewellery and the items made by master craftsmen decades ago, Mala also has two

→ 18K yellow gold Kundan. Set in peacock design. Very finely crafted enamel choker, earrings, bangles and ring with rose cut diamonds, emerald beads and seed pearls.

→ Fan palm cuff, ring and earrings of the Earth Collection, handcrafted in 18k rose gold with iolite beads and diamonds.

very different collections, all facets of her creative skills and personal interests.

The Earth range are more works of art. "So this is actually not a bracelet, it's a cuff for your hand," says Mala showing a fan palm cuff, ring and earrings from the Earth Collection, handcrafted in 18K rose gold with iolite beads and diamonds.

The level of work is extraordinary with each leaf and branch crafted. Some have an organic feel with the gold worked on to create the veins of the leaves, and bark, and others are what Mala classes as "Dali-esque" so have a sense of the surreal about them. "I like to combine East and West," says Mala. "This is more West. I feel there is so much richness in the world, you don't have to restrict yourself to one thing. Being creative allows you to play.

Then there's the Chakra Collection – gold plated silver jewellery that includes bangles and cord bracelets. The designs incorporate chakras – a term originating from Sanskrit to describe the seven main "energy centres" of the body. "This came to me in meditation," says Mala. "I meditate every morning. I teach philosophy as well. Then one day I kept getting these images. I didn't understand them, they came back repeatedly."

This led to two years of research for Mala. "And that's how this was created," she says, pointing to items from the collection.

"So this I feel is a combination of my creativity, my spiritual sense and me as a jeweller. Wearing this is about bringing balance. Not only is it beautiful, it also helps in synching the micro and the macro. So those are the three!"

→ Two line bark necklace and ring, handcrafted
in 18K yellow gold, set with aquamarines and
diamonds and strung with aquamarine beads.

↓ *Jewellery Designers*

≡ **M&R Jewellers Ltd**
19/ Floor, Siu Ying Commercial Building, 153
Queen's Road, Central
Tel: 2521 4388 (By appointment)

≡ **L'Dezen Jewellery by Payal Shah**
Rm 901, 9/F, Harbour Centre Tower 2,
8 Hok Cheung Street, Hung Hom, Kowloon
Tel: 2180 7346/7347

≡ **Butani Boutiques**
The Peninsula Hong Kong
ML7, The Peninsula Hong Kong,
Salisbury Road, Hong Kong
Tel: 2907 6928

≡ **Buxani Panjwani**
Unit 2813, 28/F, North Tower,
Concordia Plaza, 1 Science Museum Road,
Tsim Sha Tsui, Kowloon
Tel: 2722 0268

Sindhi Businesswoman Who Founded Town House

Mohini Gidumal

→ Mohini and her husband Mohan Gidumal, seated, with family members.

Mohini Gidumal is the founder of Town House. What started as a modest shop has grown into a leading wholesale and retail purveyor of luxury gifts, lifestyle accessories, and stem and table ware.

She was born Mohini Gagoomal in 1937 in the Philippines, in a second-generation Indian Sindhi family. "I love the Philippines, it's such a beautiful place," says Mrs Gidumal, over a coffee at the Foreign Correspondents Club. Her father had four daughters and was insistent that they get a good education, which included university. That was rare at the time, but he also expected his daughters to meet other Indian families with eligible sons. Other sisters married, but Mohini refused to be hurried when it came to finding a life partner. Eventually, she wed a man of her own choice in Hong Kong.

The Philippines she describes was a slow-paced, country life – socializing with other well-to-do Indian families in big houses, and beach and countryside holidays. Mrs Gidumal describes an idyllic childhood. Despite her father's humble beginnings, she wanted for nothing, living in several large houses in both Baguio and Manila. When she first arrived in India in 1955, she hated it – the noise, the crowds, and the dirt. But her view has changed over the years. She regularly visits a sister there and also returns to Manila once a year.

Mrs Gidumal's father, Gagoomal Assanmal, left India when he was 17 and earned his passage to Manila by cleaning the decks of the ship. He was one of eight sons. He started working for Pohoomal Brothers in the Philippines and later set up his own firm, G. Assanmal – a company that still bears his name. "He was a very good salesman and I think I got that from him," she says.

"Now if you notice," she says, "we take our father's first name as our surname. Most of the Indians who were settled in the Philippines, Hong Kong and Japan – they would have a general Indian name – for example Mahbubani and people would ask, yes, but which Mahbubani are you? So you had this tradition of using the father's first name. But not so much anymore."

As a young woman, Mrs Gidumal bucked the trend. Her mother wanted to impress on her daughters the need to learn to cook and sew, but it held no interest for her. Meanwhile, the sons would work with their father.

In 1961, there was house fire, and Mrs Gidumal was sent by her father to Hong Kong to shop to replace everything. One of her brothers ran the family company here and through her brother, she would meet her future husband.

"I loved Hong Kong – Hong Kong had a fight and a spirit to it. Manila was too laid back. Within three or four months I met my husband, Mohan. We were courting for nearly a year and then we got married."

Her husband was in trading and had a big showroom in Ocean Terminal. "He had a factory in Kwun Tong making the Indian style striped bedspreads. Beautiful bed spreads. So he had a showroom for his customers and I used to work there twice a week."

She was a young mother of two, her children had gone off to kindergarten and she was a bit bored. So a friend, Armis Hornameek, who specialized in Chinese antique silver, suggested that they open a shop together – which they did, a 200 square foot shop called Town House in Ocean Terminal in Tsim Sha Tsui. The name was easy to remember, they'd even installed a faux fireplace in the shop to give it a homey feel.

But while her partner knew all about silver hallmarks, Mrs Gidumal realized they needed more variety in the products they carried. So she would find silver and tableware from her husband's export business and sell that. They would go to Macau to bring antique bed headboards and Chinese antique baskets. She would also buy Chinese blue and white tile paintings from the arts and crafts shops. But her friend was less than enamoured with the path the shop was taking. "She didn't like all that rubbish in the shop," says Mrs Gidumal. So she left, and Mrs Gidumal continued on her own.

With the cruise ships coming into Ocean Terminal, she began a roaring trade in Waterford crystal, cloisonné, and then spotting an opportunity, Richard Nixon snuff bottles, when Nixon made his famous trip to China in 1972. Mrs Gidumal would liaise with two Hong Kong Chinese factories, one of which was Yuet Tung China Works out in Castle Peak. Not only did they make the snuff bottles, of which she managed to sell 5,000 to an enthused American buyer at a Frankfurt trade fair. She also sold a dinner set to singer/ entertainer Danny Kaye.

Mrs Gidumal's son, Ravi, would modernise

→ Mohini and Mohan Gidumal surrounded by children and grandchildren.

Town House and expand it beyond recognition as a Hong Kong-based distributor of international tabletop and home accessories brands. But he takes his hat off to his mother for her innate ability to sell and source beautiful products from different parts of the world.

In the years after she retired and passed the business on to her son in the 1990s, Town House has become a thriving business with seven shops in Hong Kong and a large wholesale showroom selling brands the company represents to other retailers, hotels, restaurants and companies both in Hong Kong and Macau.

The Sporting Life

The Sporting Life

Hockey and cricket are key sports for Hong Kong's South Asian community – for those who have been here for generations as well as the more recent arrivals. Their outsize role in local cricket can be seen at the Little Sai Wan Cricket Club where Indians and Pakistanis account for a sizeable share of the club's past presidents and team captains.

The love of sports doesn't end here. Volleyball and football are particularly popular among the Nepalese community, as is taekwondo and bodybuilding. "Hockey usually has been dominated by South Asian players," says longtime Hong Kong sports writer Nazvi Careem. "In cricket over the past 10 years, it has gone from mostly expatriates to mostly Pakistanis and a few Indians. If you look at the Hong Kong squad, it's now 60 per cent Pakistani guys. About half of them came from Pakistan and have already developed their skills."

→ Anshveer Singh, 9, Parasdeep Singh, 11, and Vishaldeep Singh Chahal, 11, take a break after their hockey training at Happy Valley Racecourse playground.

Something else which the Sri Lankans have brought to Hong Kong is rugby. They adopted the sport from the British and have become the second largest rugby-playing nation in Asia, after Japan. It has become a professional game with domestic leagues. The emigres in Hong Kong have brought the sport with them; they have established the Tung Chung Titans in a district where many Sri Lankans live. The team has become a social network as well as a sports team.

Support of sports from the South Asian community starts early in Hong Kong's British colonial history. Parsee entrepreneur and philanthropist Sir Hormusjee Mody put in place the foundation

→ Two Sikh men play hockey at Happy Valley Racecourse playground.

stone for the first clubhouse of the Kowloon Cricket Club on January 18, 1908. He was presented with an engraved silver trowel to mark the occasion.

A few decades later, the Indian Sikhs of the Army Depot Police would enjoy field hockey and volleyball on Stonecutters Island. While hockey and cricket dominate as the typical South Asian sports, members of clubs such as the Kowloon Cricket Club or the Indian Recreation Club, also founded more than 100 years ago, have a wide spectrum of sports to choose from.

The Nav Bharat Club, in Wan Chai, was set up in 1951 to cater to the sporting and social needs of the Indian community. It promotes hockey, squash and badminton, and has produced players who went on to represent Hong Kong at an international level in hockey and squash.

At the Pakistan Association of Hong Kong in Yau Ma Tei, there are thriving cricket teams for young men and boys, largely from the Pakistani community, though there are some Bangladeshi players as well. On a Wednesday evening, the sound of bat and ball can be heard under the lights as you come up the stairs to the club. Among the cricketers is Daniyal Bukhari, 21, who plays for the association team. The commitment both for him and other players half his age is a real one. Mr Bukhari's playing role is as a wicketkeeper batsman. His batting style is a left-hand bat. He's a role model to 11-year-old Fahad Ali, and his friend, Zakir Khan. They practise several times a week and need to balance that with their schoolwork and study of the Quran in Arabic at the Kowloon Mosque.

Fahad came to Hong Kong at the age of two and is now a primary 6 pupil at the Tong Koon District Society Fong Shu Chuen School. "My mum looks after the family and my dad does security in Kwun Tong," he says. He has one older brother and one younger sister. "When I was young," he says, "I used to watch the keeper training here and I wanted to be a keeper. So that's the wicketkeeper, the player on the fielding side who stands behind the wicket or stumps."

But Fahad has recently learned how to do off-spin – a type of finger spin bowling – so he has become more interested in the bowling side. Both boys list their Pakistani cricket heroes, but closer to home another role model is Babar Hayat, a Pakistani-born Hong Kong cricketer and current Hong Kong One Day International captain.

"So you have a mix of people, who have either come into Hong Kong, or who are born in Hong Kong," says Mr Careem. Another is Hong Kong Indian player Anshuman Rath. He was good enough to play for the Middlesex team in England last year, but due to visa issues was not permitted to stay in the UK even though the county team wanted him. Nizakat Khan is another superior player. He's a Pakistan-born Hong Kong cricketer, a right-handed batsman, who

Chapter 9 —— The Sporting Life

plays for the Hong Kong national cricket team. Mr Careem regards the national team as one of the top 20 in the world.

Local young cricketers of both genders could still do with more of an injection of funding from the government for training and to encourage talent. But a relatively new tournament in the city, the Hong Kong T20 Blitz, has acted as an opportunity for local players to see true international class, with world class players coming to Hong Kong to play for franchises.

Hongkonger Yasmin Daswani has represented Hong Kong in a variety of tournaments including the 16th Asian Games, the ICC (International Cricket Council) Women's World-Cup Qualifiers and the ACC (Asian Cricket Council) under-19s.

→ Zakir Khan hits the ball during his cricket training at the Pakistan Association of Hong Kong.

→ (Left to right) Nasrullah and Daniyal Bukhari play cricket at the Pakistan Association of Hong Kong.

She's heading to London to train to become a solicitor but was able to put her legal career on hold for a year to fulfil her dream of representing Hong Kong in the World-Cup Qualifiers. At the United Services Recreation Club in Yau Ma Tei she coaches young athletes, working on their skills as well as fitness. Both the Hong Kong Cricket Club and the KCC are developing players in their mid-20s, she says.

Ms Daswani started playing cricket in 2006 when she joined the HKCC Cavaliers. It was in fact her mum who introduced her to cricket, and trained alongside her daughter.

"I grew up in an international school," she says. "I was a third-culture kid and my mother said my brother and I needed to get in

Chapter 9 —— The Sporting Life

touch with our heritage. When I was 10 and we used to go to India for our holidays, we would play cricket with the other children in the streets."

As a girl she began training on Friday nights on how to bat and bowl. This past season she was the opening or top order batsman for the Hong Kong national cricket team.

So besides winning player of the match honours and other achievements, what does she see as the highlights? "I think probably playing in the Asian Games in 2010 in Guangzhou. It was our first taste of how it felt to be a proper athlete. But perhaps on a personal note, managing to fight my way back into the team last year. I used to be benched a lot, which was pretty gutting. I got back into the team and became opening batsman."

Over at the Quarry Bay Park no.1 football pitch, the sun is beating down on a Sunday morning, but that doesn't deter Nepalese football players from the Gurkha International Football Club (GIFC) from training on the artificial turf. As the players sweat their way around the pitch, one of the team's managers Hem Thapa explains how the club with 30 players was set up seven years ago and how they train at least twice a week.

"Some of our players are quite experienced and talented," he says. "They have previously played in professional league clubs in both Nepal and India. Some of them have also represented Hong Kong Division 2 and university teams. There are more than 30 players in our team who are currently playing for GIFC in the Yau Yee League. Our target is to motivate and encourage Nepalese youth to play and compete in the Hong Kong division league and also the Nepal Professional League."

Mr Thapa and fellow organizer Praveen Thapa have set ambitious goals for their team, hoping to propel the players to the top of the Hong Kong amateur Yau Yee League within seven years. At the end of the 2017 season, GIFC were the champions of the Yau Yee League's

4th division and have now been promoted to the 3rd.

Mr Thapa works for Gurkha International, which supplies crews out of Nepal for cruise ships and workers in security jobs in Hong Kong from the Nepalese community. Its labour force is predominantly from former Gurhka families. The company also sponsors the football team, paying for pitch bookings and the football shirts.

There are more than 20 Nepalese football teams in Hong Kong, says Mr Thapa, including women's teams. Nepalese are also keen volleyball players and take part in many tournaments here. Every year there is also an annual bodybuilding contest in the Nepalese community.

→ Students play football during a lunch break at the Islamic Kasim Tuet Memorial College.

Chapter 9 —— The Sporting Life

Gurung Niranjan has recently finished a degree in accounting and is part of the Sunday morning training at Quarry Bay. He got married four months ago. Aged 25, he jokes that he's not quite so fit on the pitch at the moment as he's put on a little weight since he joined the ranks of the happily married. "When I started playing I was midfield; back then I was pretty slim and I could run," he laughs. Hem Thapa also steps in as a goalkeeper and defence, when required, but largely leaves it to the younger players and acts as coach and organizer.

He and his fellow volunteers have worked hard to build the team, improving the players' football skills, but also keeping them on a healthy track and away from bad habits.

The aim for this team is to make it to the top of the Yau Yee League, but Mr Gurung also cites two Hong Kong Nepalese players who are already at the top of their game - Thapa Prakash who plays for the Division 1 team Citizen and Thapa Saroj, who plays in the Yau Yee League Division 1 team, HKFC Colts.

Mr Thapa explains that most of the players in the GIFC teams are construction or restaurant workers, and he feels they can cope with the heat. "Nepalese are quite strong, they don't mind, as long as they have a pitch to play football."

Mr Careem says businessman Farooq Saeed is one of the only Hongkongers who has captained Hong Kong for both cricket and hockey. Mr Saeed, 48, was Hong Kong's hockey captain for 14 years. He has represented the city in both Asia Cups and Asian Games and been an inspiration to young ethnic minority children in the teams.
Mr Saeed came to Hong Kong as a boy, but returned to Pakistan to study commerce. He recalls having to cycle to the sports ground in 40 degree heat. He later played for college and university teams as well as Pakistan's Under 19 side. Later with the Hong Kong team he attended four Asian Games, three Asia Cups and two East Asian Games, playing both hockey and cricket. In 2009, the Hong Kong team won a bronze at the East Asian Games, which Mr Saeed cites as a highlight of his career. Mr Saeed was also picked as one of the

athletes to carry the Olympic torch in 2008 and ran with the torch through Sha Tin.

Over at Kowloon Park Sports Centre on a Sunday morning, a hall full of taekwondo athletes kick in the air in unison. From age 4 up, these children are increasing their fitness but also learning self-confidence and self-defence through this martial art that has achieved Olympic status. With their cross-over white jacket fronts, the children range from beginner white belts to black. They come here every weekend for training, competitions and to hone their skills. They're all members of the Hong Kong Nepal Taekwondo Association (HKNTA), which has branches across Hong Kong.

Straight after the high kicking, the children are on the floor as

→ Farooq Saeed, a former Hong Kong cricket and hockey team captain, carries the Olympic torch through Sha Tin ahead of the Beijing Olympics in 2008.

Chapter 9 —— The Sporting Life

the instructor counts press-ups, while he also does them himself, encouraging the young athletes to keep on going.

"Every three months, the children are put through a fitness test where they have to do at least 20 push-ups," says Sudhir Kumar Gurung, the commissioner of the HKNTA. "If they do regular exercise they can do it."

As part of the "upgrading" test, the children also have to show their poomsae and kicking skills. Poomsae is a defined pattern of defence and attack motions in this Korean martial art. Taekwondo translates as "kicking and punching". In addition to the push ups, they're required to do 40-50 sit-ups.

Four instructors go through warm-up exercises before teaching the children more taekwondo techniques. "It teaches the children discipline and the young generation needs to learn about discipline," says Mr Gurung. "And it's a friendly game, unlike some other martial arts, so it's good for the mind as well."

All of the instructors volunteer their time. Mr Gurung's day job is as a chartered quantity surveyor. Thapa Teman Sing is a personnel protection officer and an instructor for the association. He explains that beginners start with a white belt and then progress through the colours to a black belt, a process that takes a minimum of 2-1/2 years. The association was established in Hong Kong in 2002 and every year it has an anniversary competition. "So we invite other associations," says Mr Gurung. "And the Hong Kong police. We're hoping to get the arena here" for the competition.

Narendra Gurung works as a project manager at Jeb International, an interior design services company. He's an ex-Gurkha soldier, who hopes some of the children he teaches can aspire to represent Hong Kong at the Olympics in taekwondo. There are regular opportunities for the children to take part in competitions and win medals and he hopes to push them to higher levels.

→ (Top) Nepali children practise Taekwondo at Kowloon Park Sports Centre.

→ (Bottom) Sudhir Kumar Gurung, the commissioner of the Hong Kong Nepal Taekwondo
   Association and instructor Narendra Gurung.

Sneha Ghale, 15, came to Hong Kong from Nepal three years ago, which is when she started taekwondo, following her father. "It helps with our physical and mental health and also with self defence, especially for the girls. I have participated in many sparring and poomsae competitions," she says. "Right now I'm red/black (belt)," she says, referring to her status just below the coveted black belt level. But she did the black belt test three months ago and will be granted her new status soon.

"I want to carry on," she says. "And I want to help the young generation."Master Dev Chandra Gurung is the chief instructor of the HKNTA and has been continuously teaching in Hong Kong for more than 20 years. "Our main focus is to give the children more awareness and training. Obviously, we have a lot of competitions, so that they can achieve, which is hopefully good for them."

Bipen Limbu, 13, came second at a recent Macau open taekwondo competition. He says he arrived one day at the Kowloon Park Sports Centre to go swimming with his father. "I happened to come to this corner for some reason," he says, pointing up the corridor. "And I saw the taekwondo class and I instantly fell in love with it. But it's not easy! After the first lesson, I came out and told my Dad that all my body my body parts were in pain, my legs were aching. But you get used to it as you go on."

Lisha Bhavnani, 14, lives in Tsim Sha Tsui. She was born here, but regularly goes to India to see relatives. "I joined taekwondo to learn self defence," she says. "As a girl it's really important for us to learn how to defend ourselves in the world. And there are a lot of skills we can use, including discipline. So we learn how to behave properly in front of others. We also learn leadership roles, how to lead other groups, and to teach the younger children about our skills."

Lisha has enjoyed the year since she started learning with the other Nepalese children and says there's a very supportive atmosphere. "I'm still learning. It's a great opportunity as I can inspire other children and show that girls are as equally strong as other people. And it's also really fun!"

On another Sunday in Happy Valley members of the Sikh community are gathering for a sports day. Children and teenagers arrive with their hockey sticks, parents arrive laden with food. Throughout the day there will be hockey matches, different kinds of races for all ages, football and even a tug of war. The event is to mark Visaki, the Sikh new year in April.

As the older players enter the grounds at the event, they each pay their respects to a man sitting in a light blue turban near the entrance. This is Kewal Singh, a coach and former Hong Kong team player.

"I came to Hong Kong in the 1970s," he says. "And in 1981 played on the under 19 team. I played for 15 years for the Hong Kong national team, also a number of times at the Asian Games."

Mr Kewal, 53, was born in Punjab but came to Hong Kong at the age of 16. He got married in 1985, and says his son is now also a good player. He coaches players from the Sikh temple between the ages of 7 and 16. The temple also has the very well established Khalsa team. Alongside his government job, Mr Singh says his only thoughts are of sport. This includes arduous relay races, and in hockey as part of the Hong Kong national team, the Asian Games and Junior World Cup qualifiers. "In 1990, I played in the Asian Games. Hong Kong didn't win as India and Pakistan were so strong."

These days, he says, there are so many sports available to children at school, which he sees as important for their health and wellbeing.

---

1. Interviews with sports writer Nazvi Careem, plus multiple interviews with former and current sportspeople across a variety of sports and South Asian communities in Hong Kong.

2. *South China Morning Post*, sports club websites.

Chapter 9 —— The Sporting Life

Chapter

10

*From Fasting
to Feasting –

South Asian
Festivals*

From Fasting to Feasting - South Asian Festivals

South Asians brought their religious and cultural festivals with them to Hong Kong. These festivals retain their significance to these communities to this day.

For Hindus, Sikhs and Jains, one of the most important holidays is Diwali, the festival of lights. It is a five-day celebration in the autumn; in 2018, it will be held from November 6-10. The main festival night of Diwali coincides with the darkest, new moon of the Hindu lunisolar month of Kartika in the Bikram Sambat calendar. It symbolises the victory of good over evil, light over darkness, knowledge over ignorance and hope over despair; people light lamps as a sign of hope and celebration. In countries with large Indian populations, lamps shine from rooftops, glow inside and outside the home and flicker around temples and other buildings.

→ Hong Kong Indians celebrate Diwali, the Hindu New Year at the Khalsa Diwan Sikh Temple in Wan Chai.

Ahead of Diwali, homes and offices are cleaned, renovated, and festooned with fragrant flowers and candles. During the holiday, the faithful put on new clothes or their best attire. Families offer prayers to Lakshmi, the goddess of prosperity. In a modern twist to tradition, firecrackers are set off. Families and friends exchange gifts and Indian confectioneries; traditional favourites including barfi – a soft, milk-based sweet – and laddu – a sphere-shaped sweet made with flour, milk and sugar. During the five days, prayers are offered at home and in the temple. In countries where Diwali is celebrated, this is also an important time for shopping.

Chapter 10 —— From Fasting to Feasting – South Asian Festivals

For the Sikh and Hindu communities of Hong Kong, Diwali is one of the most joyful events of the year. Temples are crowded with worshippers amid a rich display of light and colour. Families gather, hold lavish meals and exchange gifts. The community feels a sense of unity and joy.

"Diwali is big and we do celebrate. It's a great opportunity for families to be together," says Hong Kong comedian Vivek Mahbubani. "I would say there are different degrees of how you celebrate Diwali – you dress up and have the big Indian dinner, or you say 'hey happy Diwali, let's go out and have a meal and visit different relatives'. Back when my grandmother was alive, a lot of family members would come and visit us. But now that she's passed away, we go and visit [other] family members instead.

"You know how Chinese New Year is like a random date at the beginning of the year? Same with Diwali," he says. "It's the festival of lights. So on that night we try to light up the whole house, with candles or turning on all the lights. Basically, (we're) bringing in more energy. And we have prayers, we have dinner together. We sometimes visit family or they come and visit us. It's all about positive energy and showing respect to your elders.

"We are all vegetarian on that day. So it's very rare that you would eat meat. The tradition is that you say your prayers, eat dinner together, dress in fresh clothes – you don't want to look tired on that day. And you'll often go to the office, and say prayers to be thankful for all the good things that have happened in the year."

For the Parsees in Hong Kong it is much the same.

"Parsees enjoy eating and drinking and getting together, no matter where they live, no matter where they are. This is something they enjoy doing," says fourth generation Hongkonger Jimmy Minoo Master, of the Parsee community that traces its origins to Iran. "So as far as festivals are concerned, they will celebrate everything! They will celebrate the Chinese festivals, they will celebrate the Western

→ Diwali is a joyous festival, celebrated by Hindus, Jains, Sikhs and Nepalese Newar Buddhists.

festivals as well as our own.

"The Parsee New Year falls somewhere in the month of August, and we have an Iranian new year Nowruz, which is celebrated around March 21, the spring equinox."

Among the foods eaten during these festivals are a traditional drink called falooda, which is prepared with milk and rose water. A breakfast staple for festivals is ravo, which is prepared with suji or semolina, milk and sugar, and sev, a sweet vermicelli.

Flats and houses are decorated with chalk, passed through a metal die which imprints auspicious symbols including birds, fish, stars and butterflies. These also appear on the Parsee garas, which are intricate embroidery on sari borders. When guests arrive over the holiday, the hosts sprinkle rose water and rice and apply tili to their foreheads.

"In addition to those two festivals, we also celebrate the birth of our prophet, Zoroaster, towards the end of August. And there are a number of days each month on which the deceased are remembered," he says.

Prayer is always an important aspect of their faith and it normally precedes any festive occasion, says Jimmy. So at the time of the Parsee New Year and other festivals, there's always a prayer service before the community gets together and has cocktails and dinner. "The priest leads the prayers. Sometimes we do have additional lay priests who pray alongside our priest and it's one occasion where the community manages to get together in a single place. A community that prays together, stays together."

For Muslims in Hong Kong as all over the world, the most important festival of the year is Eid al-Fitr that marks the end of Ramadan, the Islamic holy month of fasting. It celebrates the conclusion of the 29 or 30 days of dawn-to-dusk fasting during the entire month of Ramadan. It is a day of unity and brotherhood. In order to accommodate the large number of people who attend Eid prayers at Kowloon's mosques, prayers are held at three different times in the morning, led by different imams. A total of 5,000 people offer the Eid prayers. After prayers, Muslims visit relatives and friends or hold large communal celebrations in homes, community centres or rented halls. Older people make gifts of money to children. It is a day of unity and brotherhood. Muslims clean their homes ahead of the festival. They regard Ramadan as a time of self-reflection and purification, a way to get closer to God.

The Sri Lankan community in Hong Kong celebrates several festivals. One is the Sri Lankan New Year, observed by both Sinhalese and Tamils. The date is not decided by the Gregorian calendar but by astrological calculations; it usually falls in April, beginning at the sighting of the new moon. People clean their homes and light

→ Indonesian Muslims wait the end of Ramadan in Victoria Park, Causeway Bay.

an oil lamp and begin their cultural rituals. Other festivals are to honour Buddha as most Sri Lankans are Buddhist. They celebrate the three most important events in the life of Buddha on Vesak Day, which falls in the month of May. These three events are his birth in Lumbini in Nepal; his enlightenment as the Buddha under the Bodhi tree, in Bodh Gaya in Bihar, India; and his passing at Kusinagar in Uttar Pradesh in India, which has become an important destination for Buddhist pilgrims from around the world. To mark the Vesak Festival, the Sri Lankans of Hong Kong visit temples, offer flowers, light lamps and burn incense. They sing devotional songs and offer food to devotees.

For the Nepalis of Hong Kong, an important festival is Purkha Diwas, or Ancestors Day, held at the Gurkha Cemetery in San Tin

→ Nepalese girls with traditional Kantha necklaces dance during Buddha purnima.

For the Nepalis of Hong Kong, an important festival is Purkha Diwas, or Ancestors Day, held at the Gurkha cemetery in San Tin Barracks in Yuen Long. It is a gathering of the different Gurkha clans - Gurung, Limbu, Magar, Rai, Thapa and others. It is an opportunity for younger members of the community to learn about their culture and history. In 1997, as China regained sovereignty over the territory, the British turned over the barracks to the People's Liberation Army. To make the visit these days, Nepalis must seek permission from the Commonwealth War Graves Commission and the Security Bureau of the Hong Kong government. The community uses the festival to organise photographic exhibitions and display historical records, to show the contribution of the Gurkhas in the First and Second World Wars and raise awareness of the life in their native villages in Nepal. Other festivals are Losar, celebrated by the Gurung caste, a festival

→ Devotees pray during the Behrano Ceremony, at the beginning of a Sindhi New Year.

that ushers in a new year and marks the start of spring. According to Nepalese astrology, each year is assigned a zodiac animal, and this festival marks the change from one animal to the next. Dashain is the longest and most auspicious festival for Nepalese. It is observed over a 15-day period in September and October. Houses are cleaned and beautifully decorated, as an invitation for a visit by the divine mother goddess Durga. In the past, thousands of animals were ritually slaughtered at this time of year in Nepal, but this practice has been set aside in recent years.

And Tihar is the Nepalese festival of lights, the country's second most important festival after Dashain. In Hong Kong, these festivals are sometimes celebrated in the Country Parks such as Monkey Hill.

Chapter 10 —— From Fasting to Feasting – South Asian Festivals

A Nepalese Wedding

Niranjan and Susmita

→ Niranjan and Susmita Gurung at their wedding in Nepal.

Gurung Niranjan moved to Hong Kong from Nepal five years ago. He completed a degree in accounting at a Hong Kong university last year and got married in February back in Nepal.

Niranjan, 25, describes how he had a traditional wedding, which he knew little about before his own. While he felt a bit overwhelmed at first, he was able to enjoy the day because he had been together with his wife to be, Susmita, for 10 years. He knew all the family members and friends at the event.

Unlike many marriages in India and Nepal, Niranjan's was not arranged. "Mine was choice, because I knew her from high school. So we were actually in a relationship before getting married, and both of our families are quite understanding," he says. While his and Susmita's closer family members live in Hong Kong, most of the relatives are in Nepal. "So both our families went back to Nepal in February for the wedding," which he says was a mix of Hindu and Buddhist traditions.

Niranjan describes how people from different religions are tolerated in Nepal. "I guess most Nepalese – about 80-90 per cent – are Hindu. There are also a small number of Muslims and Christians. So my family actually follows both Hindu and Buddhist rituals, a mixture of both. Originally our people were more Buddhist but since they started to live with Hindu people, I guess they borrowed some of their rituals."

So on the wedding day, Niranjan and Susmita and their families had a Hindu ceremony, but also went to Buddhist monasteries to pray to Buddha.

On the big day, Niranjan wore a conventional suit while his wife wore a traditional Hindu red sari. "I also put the tika on her forehead," he says, referring to the red dot from a paste or powder that can signify a blessing or a lifelong partnership. "In Hindu culture, once a girl gets married she has a tika on her forehead to signify that she is married."

Niranjan describes how there was plenty of food on the day, and while the guests ate their fill, he and his wife had little time for food. "What happens in Hindu traditional marriages is that the bride and groom are busy receiving tikas from the guests so we didn't get to eat as much as the guests did," he laughs.

The ceremony took place at a wedding hall.

"Some people go to the temple and then to the wedding venue, but for us we just went directly to the wedding venue and got the ceremony done there," he says.

So, how did he pop the question? Well, it turns out it's quite different in Nepalese society. He didn't. "No, I didn't actually even have to ask her, as we've known one another for so long, our parents accepted us so we didn't have a formal sit together and, you know, go ask her."

Niranjan describes how in certain respects Nepalese culture is similar to Indian culture, "in that most marriages are predominantly arranged marriages. Mostly what happens the parents try to find a suitable groom or bride for their sons and daughters. So the parents meet first, assess one another, see whether or not they're a match. And then once they decide that both of them are good, then they ask the boy and girl to meet. And if the girl and boy then agree, in most cases, they marry. In some cases they are even forced."

But for Susmita and Narinjan it was more informal. No ring, no bended knee. "But my wife now complains that I didn't propose properly to her," says Narinjan. "You know the Western way where you propose —

maybe on the first anniversary, I'll surprise her."

Vivek Mahbubani, Hong Kong comedian, on Indian Weddings

"We go to close Indian family weddings. For example, some of my cousins recently got married in India. So I went down there for a week and basically there was a different event every day. This day's for this, this day's for that. On one day you've got the bride getting henna drawn all over her body. And it's a game for the groom where she has his name somewhere hidden in the drawings. And he has to come and look for it. All these kinds of games," he says.

"Or for example, the groom has to have his clothes ripped off to kind of signify a new beginning after getting married. And I'm like, man, we grew up together, I'm not ripping your clothes off. The Indian wedding is a very big deal. It's of big significance to the family as well, welcoming someone into their family. We're proud. Let's tell the world now, let's tell the whole society. There's a huge amount of eating. If there's no food, we're not coming. On one of the days you make as much noise as you can in your house to

→ Niranjan and Susmita Gurung at the wedding ceremony with family members.

signify that you are getting married, but in
Hong Kong you have to be careful, because
your neighbour's right there."

Go Bollywood!

Karishma Sujan

→ For Karishma Sujan, Bollywood dancing is a family thing. Her mother taught her how to dance, and her brother also performs.

Every Saturday evening on Radio 3, RTHK, Karishma Sujan presents The Bollywood Show, an hour of Bollywood hits and news about Indian cinema. Karishma grew up in a family of Bollywood dancers; it's in her blood.

"I've been dancing since the age of three," she says at an RTHK studio in Kowloon Tong, while taking a break from producing the following week's programme. "Bollywood dancing is very interesting because I think it's a fusion of everything, not even just Indian. It's a fusion of hip hop, South Indian, very classical, very meaningful. Yet sometimes they have Spanish music, Arabic music and they mix it all together and that's Bollywood." And, of course, the really fun North Indian Bhangra music.

Karishma and her brother got some of their dance training from their mother, who is also a Bollywood dancer. Karishma was born in the Philippines, but was brought to Hong Kong soon afterwards. "Bollywood movies are all about 'happy', there's lots of colours, a lot of emotion, there's also a lot of crying – but generally a happy ending," she says. "So there's always a happy song at the end."

On her weekly show, Karishma will choose a theme and mix in the songs from the Bollywood movies from there. "So sometimes I do a singer, an event, the weather! I've just done 'summer' as a theme, as Bollywood has a lot of beachy summery songs. There's a lot of variety in Bollywood."

As well as English, Karishma also speaks Sindhi and Hindi. "Bollywood songs are in Hindi. So you can really learn your Hindi by listening to Bollywood songs!"

Famous Bollywood actors regularly visit Hong Kong. "They also have Bollywood nights here as well," says Karishma, who's also won plenty of Bollywood competitions over the years and taken part in Bollywood musicals. "There will be some old Bollywood songs and everyone starts screaming at the legendary classics. So I'm all about that. What they are doing now is they are taking those old songs and remaking them. So I had a show about remaking these vintage songs."

Bollywood music also mixes aspect of south Indian music. "I'm not very much in the south Indian scene," says Karishma, "as I'm north Indian." Forms of dance such as Bharatanatyam and Kuchipudi are more serious. "They come from scriptures, it's taken a lot more seriously. So when people go and watch a south Indian performance it is given a lot more respect. They pray before the performance. I love it, it's amazing, I love to go and watch it as well." In south India, they have Tollywood – so Tamil and Telugu language movies and songs.

"I recently acted in a Telugu film," says Karishma. Called Bhoo, it was shot in Hong Kong. "Sometimes we'll merge," says Karishma of Bollywood and Tollywood. "But they often have their own cinema going on. More colourful and fun than Bollywood sometimes, but it will also have more serious classical music and dancing." She is in the movie for 10 minutes playing a diva who becomes possessed in someone's dream. "I don't speak the language so I had to (struggle to) learn my lines."

When Karishma is listening at home, she prefers to choose songs based on Indian actors and actresses rather than individual singers. "So my absolute favourite, if I had to choose a singer, would be Mika Singh. Mika Singh is a Punjabi singer. His songs are amazing. He gets everyone up. He recently had a show in Hong Kong. He just gets you moving. He's probably the best live performer."

Karishma enjoys listening to songs sung by the actor Salman Khan in his movies. "His songs are very unique to him. So when he acts in a song, he sometimes sings in films now, he's very auto tuned, but they are really fun. "

Other than Khan, her choices would include: "Badshah, a rapper, he's trending right now and Kanika Kapoor, young, happy kind of singing."

So after her first foray into Tollywood acting in the movie Bhoo, does Karishma see herself doing any more acting in addition to her Bollywood radio programme?

"I can definitely see me doing more acting, but I have to be quite careful with my roles. As I come from quite a conservative family. But it's something I enjoy. If the role makes sense then I definitely would be interested, yes."

→ Indian movies available on DVD in Hong Kong, including "PK", directed by renowned Indian director Rajkumar Hirani.

↓ *Karishma on The Bollywood Show*

≡ **Radio 3, RTHK,**
Saturdays, 9.05pm-10pm.

Acknowledgements

The authors and publishers of this book wish to express their profound gratitude to the many members of the South Asian communities who gave their precious time, energy and resources to make the book possible. They gave us long interviews and written and photographic material; they welcomed us into their places of worship, community associations, shops, restaurants and other venues; and they facilitated the work of our photographer Kevin Lee. Without this warm co-operation, we would have no book. The reader will find in the different chapters the names of all those who helped us. We thank them all very much. We must also thank Ali Khan, a member of the Hong Kong Association of Registered Tour Co-ordinators. He is a Hong Kong resident of Pakistani origin with a long career as a tour guide. He used his wide network in the South Asian community to arrange introductions and meetings for us. He worked with great enthusiasm and a broad smile on his face; his help has been invaluable.

Ahmad, Buraq Islamic Store
Allah Dad Ditta
Ammar Mosque and Osman Ramju Sadick Islamic Centre
Anita Gurung
Bally Gill
Bangladesh Association of Hong Kong
Bangladesh Chamber of Commerce in Hong Kong
Captain Nam Sing Thapa Magar.
Council of Hong Kong Indian Associations
Damesh Niroshan
Daniyal Bukhari
Dewan Saiful Alam Masud
Dr. Dhiraj Gurung

Dr Narindah Pal Singh Gill

Fahad Ali

Farooq Saeed

Freedas Salon

Gaylord Indian Restaurant

Gill Sukha Singh

Gurkha Cemeteries Trust

Gurkha International Football Club

Gurung Jagat Ambu

Gurung Niranjan

Gurung Prativa

Happy Valley Hindu Temple

Hello Kitchen HK

Hem Chandra Thapa

Hong Kong Nepali Taekwondo Association

Ikram Ahmed Khan

Image Hair Salon

Indra Baraha Jwellery

Islamic Kasim Tuet Memorial College

Jagraj Singh

Jashan Celebrating Indian Cuisine

Jalalia Provision Store

Jharana Bhujel

Jimmy Minoo Master

Joanne Kwok

Justice Kemal Bokhary

Karishma Sujan

Kewal Singh

Khalsa Diwan Hong Kong

Kowloon Mosque and Islamic Centre

Kulbir Singh Dhaliwal

Kuldip Singh Uppal

Kung Yung Koon

Lal Hardasani

Liam Fitzpatrick

Lubna Farhin

MacLehose Centre

Major Balkrishna Rana

Mala Daswani

M&R Jewellery

Manakamana Nepali Restaurant

Masjid Ammer and the Osman Ramju Sadick Islamic Centre

Maxi Trading Company

Minhas Rashad

Mohini Gidumal

Mufti Muhammad Arshad

Namo Buddha Aama Samuha Hongkong

Narendra Gurung

Nazvi Careem

Nigel Collett

Nury Vittachi

OM Divya Boutique

Prativa Gurung

Praveen Thapa

Professor Malik Peiris

Rajeev Bhasin

Ray Stal

Ravi Gidumal

Ravindra Shroff

Sam's Tailor

Samina Fashion House

Serendib Restaurant

Services for Ethnic Minorities Unit, HK SKH Lady

Shalini Mahtani

Siddhababa General Store

Sikh Gurudwara

Six Star Recycle & Paper-Metal Company

Sri Lankan Buddhist Cultural Centre Hong Kong

Sudhir Gurung

Sunita Gurung

Super Angelic Hair & Beauty Salon

Susma Rana

Terry Mahmood

Thapa Teman Sing

The Incorporated Trustees of the Islamic Community Fund of Hong Kong

The Indian Chamber of Commerce Hong Kong

The Pakistan Association of Hong Kong

Time Asia

Town House

Utham Yang

Venerable Sumiththa Thero

Veronica Wong

Vivek Mahbubani

Wisewomenhk.com

Yasmin Daswani

Zakir Khan

Zubin Foundation

Photo Credits

Thanks to the following people and organisations for allowing us to use their photographs.

Unless otherwise stated, all photographs were taken by Kevin On Man Lee between March and July 2018.

P15, 16, 18 Tai Kwun (Central Police Station)

P20, 106, 108 Ko Tim-keung

P21 Dr. Joseph Ting Sun-pao

P29, 119, 120 Hong Kong and Khalsa Diwan (Sikh Temple)

P48, 186, 299, 301 South China Morning Post

P52 Liam Fitzpatrick

P56, 58 Shalini Mahtani

P110, 113 (Top), 136 Annemarie Evans

P113 (Bottom) Kemal Bokhary

P138 Gill Sukha Singh

P146 Col. Lavender

P147, 148, 150, 153 Lieutenant-Colonel Nigel Collett

P158, 161 Major Balkrishna Rana

P168, 171 Prativa Gurung

P182, 185 Nury Vittachi

P194, 200 Ikram Ahmed Khan

P202, 205 Dewan Masud

P220, 221, 233 (Top two), Jashan Celebrating Indian Cuisine

P217, 219 Jo Jo Indian Cuisine

P270, 273, 275 Mala Daswani, M&R Jewellers Ltd.

P276, 279 Ravi Gidumal

P291 Farooq Saeed

P306, 309 Niranjan Gurung

P310 Karishma Sujan

HOW SOUTH ASIAN HELPED TO MAKE HONG KONG
– History, Culture, Profiles, Food, Shopping

Author   → Mark O'Neill, Annemarie Evans
Photographer   → Kevin On Man Lee
Coordinator   → HARTCO
English Editor   → William Kazer
Photo Editor   → Anne Lee
Designer   → Michelle Mak

Published by Joint Publishing (H.K.) Co., Ltd.
20/F., North Point Industrial Building, 499 King's Road,
North Point, Hong Kong

Printed by Elegance Printing & Book Binding Co., Ltd.
Block A, 4/F., 6 Wing Yip Street, Kwun Tong, Kowloon, Hong Kong

Distributed by SUP Publishing Logistics (HK) Ltd.
3/F., 36 Ting Lai Road, Tai Po, N. T., Hong Kong

First Published in July 2018
ISBN 978-962-04-4375-6

三聯書店
http://jointpublishing.com

JPBooks.Plus
http://jpbooks.plus

 三聯書店 (香港) 有限公司
Joint Publishing (H.K.) Co., Ltd.

 聯合出版集團